Challenging Behavior and Developmental Disability

Challenging Behavior and Developmental Disability

JEFF SIGAFOOS
The University of Texas at Austin, Austin, Texas

MICHAEL ARTHUR
The University of Newcastle, Newcastle, Australia

and

MARK O'REILLY
The University of Texas at Austin, Austin, Texas

W
WHURR PUBLISHERS
LONDON AND PHILADELPHIA

© 2003 Whurr Publishers Ltd
First published 2003
by Whurr Publishers Ltd
19b Compton Terrace
London N1 2UN England and
325 Chestnut Street, Philadelphia PA 19106 USA

British Library Cataloguing in Publication Data

A catalogue record for this book
is available from the British Library.

ISBN 1 86156 378 7

Typeset by Adrian McLaughlin, a@microguides.net
Printed and bound in the UK by Athenæum Press Ltd, Gateshead,
Tyne & Wear.

Contents

Acknowledgements

Appreciation is extended to Dr Vanessa A. Green for her insightful comments on and careful editing of a previous draft of this book.

Some sections in Chapters 6 and 7 are based on and adapted from training materials written by Jeff Sigafoos for Project Exceptional MN, St Paul, Minnesota. We are grateful to the Editor of Project Exceptional MN, Dr Cindy Croft, for permission to adapt this material.

Preface

Behavior is challenging when its frequency and severity make it dangerous, destructive, harmful, disruptive, or otherwise unacceptable. Common types of challenging behavior include aggression, property destruction and other disruptive acts, self-injury, stereotyped movements and extreme tantrums. Individuals with developmental disabilities are two to three times more likely to have challenging behaviors when compared with typically developing peers. Up to 40% of people with developmental disabilities may have one or more forms of challenging behavior. The prevalence and forms of challenging behavior vary with type and severity of disability and with limitations in communication, social and other adaptive behavior skills. Episodes of challenging behavior often begin early in life and, in the absence of effective intervention, are likely to persist well into adulthood. Left untreated, challenging behaviors can have serious and long-term negative consequences. In extreme cases, they may even be life-threatening.

From this brief overview of some basic facts it should be painfully obvious why the treatment of challenging behavior is a major priority in developmental disability services. Less obvious, perhaps, is how to explain these facts and what can be done to reduce and prevent challenging behaviors. Our book aims to give an overview of the evidence in four key areas so as to give you – the reader – a better understanding of challenging behavior as well as a better understanding of how to begin the often difficult and ongoing process of assessment and intervention. The key areas covered in this book correspond to its four major sections: Conceptualizing Challenging Behavior; Fundamental Issues in Service Provision; Assessment of Challenging Behavior; and Treatment and Prevention.

To begin the process of supporting individuals with developmental disabilities and challenging behaviors it is important to have a systematic approach for defining what is and what is not challenging behavior. By this we mean more than simply deciding whether this or that particular act should be classified as a challenging behavior – although this is certainly a necessary component in the quest towards better understanding and more effective treatment. What is also needed is a socially and empirically valid conceptualization of challenging behavior. It is important to have some sort of framework – a theory if you will – of challenging behavior that integrates what is known about behavior and human nature in general and one that can account for why and how certain factors increase the risk of challenging behavior in people with developmental disabilities. This is the aim of the initial three chapters that constitute Part 1 of the book.

In Part 1 we will take challenging behavior as our dependent variable. It is what we seek to understand and measure, as well as reduce, replace, modify and accommodate. No advances can be made in understanding and treatment without reliable and valid definitions of the dependent variable. This requirement is equally important to the researcher, who aims to make general statements about the nature of challenging behavior, and to the clinician, whose mission is treatment. The researcher asks: What type of behavior is it? How should it be classified and categorized? How is it different from or similar to other behaviors that we call adaptive or functional? What basic principles and mechanisms explain the development and persistence of challenging behavior? What independent variables influence the frequency and severity of challenging behavior? And so on. Answers to these types of questions are critical to developing new and more effective treatments.

The clinician is interested in these types of questions too, but must also decide how best to treat challenging behavior in specific cases. The clinician asks: What behaviors should be targeted for intervention? What factors, be they biological, developmental, environmental or medical, are relevant to my client's behavior problems? Can these factors be altered to reduce the likelihood of challenging behavior? Clinicians are understandably under some pressure to figure out what intervention strategies are indicated and what can be done to ensure that the treatment plan is implemented effectively. These more applied issues are covered in Parts 2 through 4 of the book. The chapters in these parts examine ethical and quality of life issues, the relation between assessment and intervention, and of course treatment and prevention strategies.

In this book we seek to explore the social and the empirical sides of challenging behavior in people with developmental disabilities. Our firm belief, based on our reading of the scientific literature and our experiences as researchers and clinicians, is that effective treatment of challenging behavior requires more than a thorough knowledge of effective strategies and a high level of clinical skill in implementing these strategies. Although one could not even hope to fulfill the clinician's mission without the requisite knowledge and skills, those who take on the role of researcher or clinician will be more effective if they first understand the nature of challenging behavior and the basic scientific principles that underlie assessment and intervention.

This book does not therefore aim to provide a comprehensive review of specific techniques. It is not a "how-to" book nor is it an exhaustive review of the literature. Instead, this book aims to present the major principles that underlie the existing literature and to weave these principles into a coherent system for conceptualizing challenging behavior, undertaking assessments, and developing treatments. And yet there is enough literature review to satisfy the emerging scholar and enough technique embedded in the content to satisfy the clinician looking for new ideas and strategies. In this sense, the book will assist emerging scholars in gaining familiarity with the field and assist clinicians in developing an understanding of the basic principles that underlie assessment and intervention.

In the end, we hope that this attempt to create a coherent system from the many lines of work that have delved into the nature, assessment and treatment of challenging behavior will prove useful to graduate students, beginning researchers and clinicians in education, psychology, speech pathology, occupational therapy, social work and related disciplines. What the reader may learn, as we ourselves have learned, is that while this book is about challenging behavior in people with developmental disabilities, it is also a book about human nature. People with developmental disabilities are first and foremost human beings. Their behavior, be it adaptive or maladaptive, is human behavior; influenced by past and present circumstances and capable of change and development. To understand challenging behaviors in people with developmental disabilities is to understand human nature.

PART 1

CONCEPTUALIZING CHALLENGING BEHAVIOR

CHAPTER 1

Defining and describing challenging behavior

Introduction

What is challenging behavior? It is a seemingly simple and straightforward question. In fact for many readers the question is probably so self-evident that its answer hardly warrants a paragraph let alone an entire chapter. Some might even consider the term "challenging behavior" to be nothing more than a trendy euphuism for behaviors more commonly known by terms such as aggression, property destruction, self-injury or tantrums. If pressed, you would no doubt be able to add a long list of more specific acts to each of these broad classes. The list for aggression, for example, might include hitting, kicking, biting or scratching another person. In general discourse, this level of specificity would suffice.

In contrast to general discourse, the questions of interest to the researcher and clinician require greater attention to empirical evidence. It is therefore critical to integrate what is known about challenging behavior into a sound conceptualization of challenging behavior. A useful conceptualization might develop from an attempt to address some of the more fundamental questions about challenging behavior. How is it defined? What specific types or forms of behavior are covered by the term and how common are these forms? Can these various forms be classified in some sensible way? For it to have any use at all, the general conceptualization emerging from a consideration of these questions and issues must of course match the reality of the behavior shown by individuals. Addressing these questions and issues is the aim of this chapter.

With this aim in mind, the chapter begins with a description of the population under consideration. This is followed by a brief consideration of terminology. We then turn from a general consideration of terminology to the more specific definition of the term challenging behavior. After this, we examine the prevalence of various types and forms of challenging behaviors in people with developmental disabilities and how these

3

behaviors have been classified or conceptualized. All of this lays the groundwork for describing challenging behavior at the individual level, which is the critical first step in any systematic approach to assessment and treatment.

Developmental disability

No two people are alike and no two people with developmental disability are alike. To acknowledge that individuals with developmental disabilities can present with a wide range of individual characteristics, abilities, skills, personalities, wants and needs is to begin to understand the heterogeneous nature of the term developmental disability. It is, however, equally important to acknowledge the many important characteristics shared by people with developmental disabilities. It is these shared characteristics that define the condition and distinguish people with developmental disabilities from those without.

Developmental disability is an umbrella term that covers a number of more specific conditions all of which have a major impact on development, learning and behavior. Under this umbrella are included people with intellectual, sensory and/or physical impairments. Their impairments arise from various causes, conditions and disorders. Mental retardation, autism and cerebral palsy are perhaps the most common examples, but there are literally hundreds of more specific syndromes that can cause a developmental disability. An important text edited by Christopher Gillberg and Gregory O'Brien (2000) describes a number of developmental disability syndromes, including Angleman, Cornelia de Lange, Down, Fragile-x, Lesch-Nyhan, Prader-Willi, Rett, Smith-Magenis and Williams syndromes. Our concern, at this point, is not with any unique aspects of the many and various syndromes and conditions, but rather with the shared characteristics that bring all of these syndromes and conditions under the developmental disability umbrella.

A developmental disability is both severe and chronic (Batshaw, 1997). In fact the severity must be of such magnitude that the person experiences substantial limitations in functioning. The qualifier "substantial limitations" means that the person has major deficits in three or more areas of adaptive behavior functioning. These areas include (1) self-care skills, (2) language acquisition, (3) learning ability, (4) mobility, and (5) the capacity for independent living, which includes working independently, managing domestic, personal and financial affairs, and more generally negotiating the demands of daily life. The term chronic means that these limitations are not temporary or acute; rather they are enduring and persistent. While good interventions can lead to significant improvements in functioning and a higher quality of life, the condition itself is thought to be permanent.

However much one might wish, a child does not grow out of a developmental disability. Indeed, developmental disabilities emerge during the early developmental period – prior to age 5 – and the more severe forms are often highly obvious from birth. In some cases the nature and extent of the disability may not become fully appreciated until later in life, but in all cases the disability begins to affect the person's development, learning and behavior prior to reaching maturity at 22 years of age.

The above description provides a definitional answer to the question, "What is a developmental disability?" It is not sufficient for understanding developmental disability, however, because it omits two important points. As we shall see in Chapters 2 and 3, these two points must be taken into account in any attempt to explain challenging behavior in people with developmental disabilities. The first point is this: Developmental disabilities result from neurological conditions, such as mental retardation, autism, cerebral palsy or epilepsy (Graziano, 2002). While the exact nature and cause of the neurological disorder is not always clear, the underlying basis is clearly organic or biological. The second point is that the underlying neurological condition results in delayed, disordered or impaired development, learning and behavior.

The fact that developmental disabilities stem from neurological disorder does not mean that social and psychological factors are not important in the development and persistence of challenging behavior. Nor does this fact mean that educational and behavioral treatments are futile in the treatment of challenging behavior. On the contrary, psychosocial factors can greatly determine the expression of challenging behavior. More generally, a host of environmental factors can influence the extent to which the individual's developmental disability is more or less severe and the extent to which it leads to handicap. A girl may be unable to walk because of cerebral palsy, but she will be less handicapped if she can be taught how to use a wheelchair and if her physical environment is made wheelchair accessible.

Development, learning and behavior are influenced to varying degrees by a complex interaction of numerous bio-psychosocial variables (Sigafoos, Einfeld and Parmenter, 2001). Given the underlying neurological basis of developmental disability, however, one might expect the biological arm of the bio-psychosocial triad to act as a constraint. This constraint may influence the extent to which the substantial limitations in functioning experienced by people with developmental disabilities can be overcome by intervention. Biological factors do not, however, constrain the extent to which the person's limitations can be accommodated by an accepting and tolerant society. In addition, the extent to which biological factors might constrain intervention efforts is unknown and can perhaps only be discovered by continually pushing the limits of existing treatments and seeking new and more effective interventions. Still, the extent to which biological factors influence and drive challenging behavior will no doubt have important implications for assessment (Chapter 6), intervention (Chapter 7) and prevention (Chapter 8).

Terminology

Many terms and definitions have been applied to challenging behaviors. Some of the more widely used and contemporary terms include aberrant behavior, disturbed, disruptive or disordered behavior, excess or excessive behavior, maladaptive behavior, and problem behavior or severe problem behavior. Each of these can be considered synonymous, but in recent years the term challenging behavior has become more firmly established in the literature. Part of this shift in terminology no doubt reflects changing sensibilities and political correctness.

Still, the term challenging behavior does seem to have some advantages. It is fairly neutral and does not imply any particular theoretical orientation or explanation. It does not imply that the behavior is abnormal or unusual (i.e. aberrant) when in fact it may be quite common in specific subpopulations and under certain conditions. It does not imply that the behavior is maladaptive, when in fact some challenging behaviors could be quite adapted to the environment. It does not imply that the major issue is too much (excessive) behavior when frequency of behavior may be less important than severity in some cases.

In these respects, the term problem behavior also has considerable merit. It too is fairly neutral and descriptive without implying any particular theoretical orientation. One drawback, however, is that this term has wider connotations, which do not clearly limit it sufficiently for our specific purposes. There are many problems and many types of problematic behavior – illiteracy, crime and drug abuse are problems – but we are concerned with certain types of persistent patterns of behaviors that are highly prevalent in, but by no means exclusive to, individuals with developmental disabilities. In a 1994 book chapter, Hazel Qureshi makes a similar point about the wider connotations of the terms behavior problems and behavior disturbance (pp. 18–19). Qureshi notes that these terms have been associated with the field of emotional and behavioral disorders, which tends to focus on a wider range of problem behaviors in students with more mild cognitive and learning difficulties. We are concerned with a more precise class of behaviors and with individuals who have developmental disabilities.

Definition

For our purposes then, the term challenging behavior seems best suited provided we can define it in some way as to distinguish it from other terms. Challenging behaviors are – as we noted in the Preface – destructive, harmful, disruptive or otherwise unacceptable behaviors that occur with sufficient frequency and/or severity to be of major concern. The behaviors are challenging not only because they are destructive, harmful, disruptive or otherwise unacceptable, but also because they are frequent and/or severe. Challenging behaviors are pervasive and persistent, not sporadic. Indeed, challenging behaviors often appear to be the only, or at least the most dominant, responses in the individual's repertoire, but this is probably only because other non-challenging behaviors often pale in comparison. Challenging behaviors tend to stand out against the background of other less noxious behaviors.

But challenging behaviors should not be seen solely in terms of being a feature of the individual who engages in the behavior. Rather, as Lowe and Felce (1995) explain, the problem is:

> equally shared by those who need to understand and respond to it. Thus the degree of challenge depends not only on the nature of the behavior, but also on the ability of others to tolerate, change, or minimize the consequences of it. (p. 118)

This definition of challenging behavior and its elaboration allows for considerable discretion, which is necessary because we are dealing with degrees of human behavior, not absolutes. Whether an act is considered challenging behavior or not will depend on someone's or some group's judgment. How frequent is too frequent? How severe is too severe? How harmful or destructive must it be? What is and is not acceptable? When is a concern major? When is treatment necessary? As the Lowe and Felce (1995) quote reminds us, whether an act is considered challenging or not will also depend on the extent to which others can tolerate, change or minimize the consequences of the behavior.

There will no doubt be many borderline cases, specific acts committed by specific individuals, that will create uncertainly and considerable debate as to whether or not the behavior should be defined as challenging and whether or not it warrants treatment. No definition, no matter how comprehensive or precise, will eliminate the need for professionals to use their clinical judgment. This degree of fuzziness does not mean that the term is indefinable nor should it drive clinicians into a state of paralysis by analysis. One could become so mired in definitional technicalities as to question whether there is even anything to define. This, however, ignores the fact that there are so many obvious examples of behaviors that are clearly challenging and in need of treatment.

We therefore confine ourselves to serious problems that are of high priority for treatment. This enables us to avoid the dilemma of borderline cases that might be viewed as a problem by some observers, but by no means all. By our definition, challenging behaviors are always serious and their treatment is always a high priority.

Included is the 4-year-old child with severe autism whose aggressive acts leave his parents scratched and bruised at the end of each day; the 11-year-old boy with multiple disabilities who bashes his head on the floor hundreds of times a day causing bruising and bleeding; the 18-year-old girl with cerebral palsy who screams so often and so loudly that her teachers are unable to hear themselves speak; and the 23-year-old man with profound intellectual disability who routinely tips over tables and chairs causing extensive damage to property.

Faced with these patterns of behaviors, there is little doubt that most parents, teachers and clinicians would view these acts as challenging behaviors in need of treatment. These are the types of acts that meet our definition of challenging behavior. It is these types of behaviors that are frequently identified in people with developmental disabilities and considered to be challenging.

Indeed there appears to be an emerging general consensus on the types of behaviors that are considered challenging to those who must understand and respond to them. Along these lines, Lowe and Felce (1995) obtained data on 92 people with developmental disabilities. Data were collected by interviewing caregivers on the frequency and severity of 13 types of potentially challenging behaviors. Numerous specific behaviors were rated as major behavioral challenges depending on their frequency. Three types of behaviors (physical aggression, disturbing noises and temper tantrums) were consistently judged to represent severe management problems if they occurred with sufficient frequency. In contrast, elopement (i.e. wandering away) was always considered a severe management problem even if it was infrequent and five other behaviors (self-injury, destructiveness, night-time disturbances, objectionable personal habits and antisocial behavior) were judged to be difficult to manage even if relatively infrequent.

Lowe and Felce (1995) compared their data to other studies that have documented the types of challenging behaviors in people with developmental disabilities. They reference Emerson et al. (1988), for example, who reported percentages for several types of challenging behaviors in a sample of 31 individuals already identified as needing treatment for their problem behaviors. A full 81% were referred for treatment because of severe aggression to others, 52% for property destruction and 26% for self-injury; followed by non-compliance (16%), running away (16%), smearing feces (16%), and screaming (10%). These data suggest that certain types of behaviors are consistently viewed as challenging, at least among staff who care for people with developmental disabilities. Roughly, these behaviors could be classified into the following major types: Aggression, self-injury, elopement, and other destructive/disturbing behaviors.

However, this emerging consensus is based on the degree of management difficulty as perceived by caregivers and referral to treatment. While these are clearly legitimate ways to identify behaviors that are or should be defined as challenging, there is potential danger in such approaches. The potential danger is that these approaches could neglect or discount challenging behaviors that do not impact caregivers or are not referred for treatment. An example is stereotyped movement disorders, which may negatively affect development and learning without necessarily representing a significant management problem for caregivers (Berkson and Davenport, 1962).

Care providers, be they parents, teachers or clinicians, will almost certainly have varying degrees of tolerance for different behaviors and their lines of referral for treatment will almost certainly depend to some extent on factors other than what is in the client's best interest. A teacher who is unaware that frequent hand mouthing can cause significant skin breakdown and increase the risk of infection, for example, may simply tolerate the behavior rather than making a referral for treatment. A caregiver who believes that the tantrums are a normal part of development may not report nor seek treatment for their autistic child's frequent tantrums, even though they are a serious management problem. Such factors no doubt influence the identification of behaviors that should be defined as challenging, which will in turn affect prevalence figures. The influence that such factors exert in any given survey into the nature and extent of challenging behavior is for the most part unknown.

Prevalence

Challenging behaviors are not unique to individuals with developmental disabilities, but they are at least two to three times more common in this population than in people without developmental disabilities (Einfeld and Tonge, 1996; Parmenter et al., 1998). Why this is so will be explored in Chapters 2 and 3. For now we confine ourselves to the task of getting a feel for the size and structure of the problem. How many do what? Is challenging behavior a problem shared by many people with developmental disabilities or is it relatively rare? Are there any common types and forms of challenging behavior or are there as many forms of challenging behavior as there are people with challenging behavior?

A number of studies have sought to estimate the prevalence of challenging behavior in people with developmental disabilities. The results of such studies could be expected to provide some indication of the magnitude of the problem as well as an inventory of common types and forms of challenging behavior that have been documented in people with developmental disabilities. The reality, however, is that different studies tend to yield widely differing results. Consider the fact that prevalence estimates have ranged from a low of 2% to a high of over 40% and even as high as 70% in some studies (e.g. Chung et al., 1996; Griffin et al., 1987; Jacobson, 1990; Qureshi, 1994).

At a minimum this wide range of prevalence figures makes it difficult to know the true size of the problem. Some might even infer that there is no true prevalence figure, perhaps because challenging behavior is neither a valid construct nor a meaningful dependent variable. We believe otherwise. Much of the variability from study to study reflects differences in the size and characteristics of the samples and in the survey methodology. One obvious reason why prevalence estimates could vary widely from study to study is that the individuals included in one study might differ on average and in some important way from individuals surveyed in another study. Comparing groups with markedly different prevalence figures might therefore enable one to identify potential risk factors for challenging behaviors. Chapter 2 will review risk factors for challenging behavior. For now, it is sufficient to note that differences in the composition and size of the sample and difference in how the sample was selected will no doubt influence the obtained (as opposed to the true) prevalence figure. This is because a particular sample, even if large and randomly selected, may not necessarily be representative of the population from which it was drawn.

In addition, the typical procedure in many of these prevalence studies is to give caregivers a list of challenging behaviors or a definition of challenging behavior and ask them to indicate whether each behavior on the list or any behavior meeting the definition is present or absent; frequent or severe. Researchers do not always use the same list or definition and so the results may be influenced by the specific behaviors used as examples as well as how survey respondents interpret the definition. The consistency of interpretation, or inter-informant reliability, is not always assessed in survey research of this type. In terms of controlling for such potential influences, some studies will do a better job than others. If we assume that there is in fact an underlying true prevalence figure, then better studies should yield better estimates of this figure. Total population surveys that use reliable instruments to identify clear cases of challenging behavior would seem better for this purpose than studies of smaller subpopulations using instruments of unknown reliability.

The British Prevalence Survey

Some of the best work into the prevalence of challenging behavior has come from a group of researchers in the United Kingdom. This group conducted a major survey in 1988, the results of which were disseminated in a series of journal articles and book chapters (Kiernan and Qureshi, 1993; Kiernan, Reeves and Alborz, 1995; Qureshi and Alborz, 1992). Numerous aspects of the research program are exemplary and the resulting figures would therefore be expected to provide a more accurate estimate of the prevalence of challenging behavior.

Before highlighting the major findings from the British team, it will be instructive to take a look at those aspects of their survey methodology that make it exemplary. First, the scope of the survey was huge. It covered the total population of people receiving mental retardation services in seven large health districts in the North West of England. Second, in 1995, two of these seven areas participated in a replication/follow-up survey that provided an important check on the reproducibility of the 1988 findings (Emerson et al., 2001). Third, the survey focused on major types and clear examples of challenging behavior. These were "aggressive, self-injurious, destructive, and 'other' difficult, disruptive, or socially unacceptable behavior" (Emerson et al., 2001, p. 80). Fourth, the researchers demonstrated good reliability for their data collection instruments, suggesting that there was consistent interpretation of the definition of challenging behavior by informants. Fifth, they implemented an extensive three-stage process to identify cases of challenging behavior. Together these features make this one of the best available studies into the prevalence of challenging behaviors in people with developmental disabilities.

We can now turn to the major findings from the British team. Given our aim to estimate the size of the problem and develop an inventory of common types and forms of challenging behavior, we confine ourselves to overall prevalence figures for each major type of challenging behavior. It is sufficient for this purpose to consider only the more extensive 1988 data set. The 1995 results are consistent with the 1988 findings given any reasonable margin for error. As one might expect in so extensive a study, there are many nuances to the data and so we will return to a more detailed examination of the results when we consider risk factors in Chapter 2.

Across the seven areas, the British team screened a total of 4,200 people with mental retardation for challenging behaviors. From this total population, 694 individuals were identified as having challenging behavior according to the definition used by this team, and we have already noted that their definition and screening procedures were comprehensive, reliable and focused on clear-cut instances. Dividing the number of people identified (694) by the total population (4,200) and multiplying this number by 100 gives the percentage of people from the total population with challenging behavior, which in this case turns out to be 16.5%. This then is the overall prevalence for all seven areas. But what about the range of prevalence figures across the seven areas? The seven prevalence figures are remarkably similar, ranging from 15 to 17.3%. This narrow range suggests that the overall estimate is a good one.

When the people with challenging behavior are identified within a population, we can ask what types of behaviors are most common. Among those individuals identified in 1988 as showing challenging behavior, the British team reported that most (72%) had "other" difficult, disruptive, or socially unacceptable behaviors. This was followed by aggression (42%), destructive behavior (30%), and self-injury (27%). An interesting issue is the extent to which individuals were specialists in one type of challenging behavior (John only does aggression, never self-injury) or generalists (Mary has both aggression and self-injury). The 1988 data indicate that while 49% showed only one type of challenging behavior, one-third showed two types, 15% showed three types and 3% showed all four general types, that is aggression, self-injury, destructive behaviors, and "other" challenging behavior. Roughly half would therefore appear to be specialists and the other half were of course generalists. This suggests that the more general term challenging behavior is a good descriptor given the tendency for individuals to present with multiple types, and as we shall see next, multiple forms of challenging behaviors.

Within these four general types or classes (aggression, self-injury, destructive behaviors, and "other" challenging behavior), we can also ask what specific forms or topographies are prevalent. Here the follow-up data from 1995 provide good estimates. Based on the figures from the 1995 survey as reported by Emerson et al. (2001, pp. 84–5), we have created a table (Table 1.1) showing the prevalence of specific forms or topographies within each of the major types of challenging behavior. For this table, destructive behavior has been included under "other" challenging behavior because details on the specific forms of this type of challenging behavior were not collected in the 1995 survey.

Scanning down each column gives a rank ordering – from most-to-least prevalent – of the specific topographies identified within each major class. Of the individuals identified as showing aggression, for example, 75% were said to hit others with their hands. This most common form of aggression was followed by verbal abuse (60%), hitting others with objects (41%), and so on. Common forms of self-injury included hitting one's own head with a hand or other body part (47%), followed by biting oneself (45%), hitting head with objects (42%) and so on down the list.

Table 1.1 Prevalence of specific forms or topographies of challenging behaviors

Aggression (directed at others)	Self-injury (directed at self)	Other
Hit with hand (75%)	Hit head with hand/ body part (47%)	Non-compliance (69%)
Verbal abuse (60%)	Bite (45%)	Tantrums (54%)
Hit with object (41%)	Hit head with/against objects (42%)	Repetitive pestering (46%)
Mean/cruel (34%)	Hit body with hand/ body part (35%)	Destructive (33%)
Scratch (27%)	Hit body with/against objects (27%)	Screaming (31%)
Pull hair (23%)	Pinch/scratch (19/20%)	Runs away (28%)
Pinch (20%)	Pica (eats inedible objects) (19%)	Over active (27%)
Bite (16%)	Stuff fingers in body openings (12%)	Stealing (19%)
Other aggression (8%)	Polydipsia (excessive drinking) (11%)	Sexually delinquent (19%)
	Trichotillomania (pulls out hair (11%)	Smearing feces (8%)
	Bruxism (teeth grinding) (7%)	Stripping (7%)
	Self-induced vomiting (4%)	Other forms (22%)
	Aerophagia (swallow air) (1%)	
	Other self-injury (10%)	

Source: Based on Emerson et al. (2001).

One could view Table 1.1 as an inventory of the most common forms of behaviors identified as challenging in people with developmental disabilities. It would be wise to view this as a tentative inventory, however, because it is based on the smaller 1995 survey, which covered only two of the seven areas and as such it was based on data obtained from only 264 (rather than the larger seven-region pool of 694) individuals with challenging behavior.

Other prevalence studies

Much progress can be made in understanding challenging behavior from the steady accumulation of good survey data, such as that obtained in the 1988 and 1995 British surveys. Still it would be wise to avoid placing too much stock in the results from one or two studies no matter how good the methodology. The 1998 and 1995 British studies are exemplary, but they are also tied to a specific geographic region and specific informants. Confidence in the generality of those data would be improved if the results could be replicated in other geographic regions and populations.

Fortunately there are other total population studies that can serve as a basis for comparison, although these other studies tend to be less comprehensive in that they focused on aggression or self-injury and not on challenging behavior in general.

Sigafoos et al. (1994) obtained data on aggressive behavior in a total population of 2,412 individuals with developmental disabilities in Queensland, Australia. In 1992, when the survey was conducted, 11% (261 out of 2,412) were identified with at least one form of aggressive behavior. The specific forms of aggressive behaviors among these 261 individuals were recorded and rank ordered in terms of the percentage showing each form of aggression. The resulting list is shown in the left column of Table 1.2. Data from the 1995 British survey (Emerson et al., 2001) are in the right column to facilitate comparison.

Table 1.2 Comparison of the prevalence of specific forms of aggressive behaviors in the Queensland and British surveys

1992 Queensland survey	1995 British survey
Hits others with closed or open hand (68%)	Hits others with hand (75%)
Pushes others (64%)	Verbal abuse (60%)
Uses threatening gestures (59%)	Hits others with objects (41%)
Verbal abuse (58%)	Mean/cruel (34%)
Throws objects at others (46%)	Scratches others (27%)
Forcibly takes objects from others (42%)	Pulls other's hair (23%)
Scratches others (41%)	Pinches others (20%)
Kicks others (37%)	Bites others (16%)
Pull other's hair (36%)	Other forms of aggression (8%)
Uses objects as weapons (29%)	
Pinches others (28%)	
Bites others (27%)	
Spits on others (19%)	
Chokes others (10%)	

The match is not identical, but it is encouraging that similar forms of aggressive behaviors were commonly identified in both studies. The greater number of topographies in the Queensland side of the list is no doubt related to the fact that Sigafoos et al. gave informants a checklist of 14 aggressive behaviors, rather than a comprehensive definition of challenging behavior as in the British survey.

In addition to similarities in the topographies of aggressive behaviors identified, the results of the two studies are comparable in a number of other important respects. The overall prevalence figure reported in the Queensland study (11%), for instance, is comparable to that of the 1988 British survey (16.5%). A direct comparison is not possible of course, but the two prevalence figures are consistent when one takes into account the fact that a significant number of individuals in both populations showed multiple types of challenging behavior. In the Queensland study, a full 34% of those identified with aggression also engaged in self-injury and 30% showed aggression and property destruction. Among those identified as showing aggression, multiple forms were more the rule than the exception. In Queensland, 80% of the 261 individuals showed three or more of the topographies of aggressive behaviors listed in the left column of Table 1.2. The similarity of this finding to the 1995 British data is striking. Emerson et al. (2001) reported that: "Overall, 79% ... who showed ... aggression showed two or more forms of specific aggressive behaviors" (p. 83).

Results from the Sigafoos et al. (1994) survey are also consistent with, but not identical to data from other prevalence surveys of aggressive behaviors. Russell and Harris (1993), for instance, studied 78 facilities for children and adults with developmental disabilities in a British health district. They reported an overall prevalence rate of 17.6%. This higher figure might reflect the fact that their definition of aggressive behavior includes acts that Sigafoos et al. (1994) classified as property destruction. That is, Russell and Harris included "violence towards objects" as a type of aggressive behavior, whereas Sigafoos et al. (1994) only included acts directed towards other people. The most common topographies of aggressive acts in the Russell and Harris sample were very similar to those identified in the Queensland sample, including punching, slapping and pushing/pulling others, followed by pinching, kicking, scratching, biting, although they identified head-butting as a distinct form of aggression, which was not a major form of aggression in the Queensland study.

When focused on aggressive behaviors then, we start to see a consistency among studies of total populations in terms of overall prevalence and common forms. This consistency points to an emerging body of reliable knowledge. Does the same hold when we turn our attention to self-injury?

Oliver, Murphy and Corbett published data relevant to this question in a 1987 issue of the *Journal of Mental Deficiency Research*. Details of the study also appeared in a 1993 book chapter (Murphy et al., 1993). Their study focused on the prevalence and forms of self-injurious behavior (SIB) among individuals with mental retardation (IQ < 70) in a single UK health region. Eight hundred and seventy SIB cases were referred to the project and detailed interviews were completed in March 1984 and April 1985 to identify 616 cases that met their definition for having SIB. Complete data were available for 596 of these 616 people. Separate prevalence estimates were calculated for sub-samples of this population based on age and where the person received services. The prevalence of SIB was estimated at 12% or 304 of the 2,532 people who lived in institutional settings in that particular region. The prevalence estimates were much lower for adults who did not live in institutions (3%) and for younger children in schools

(3–4%), but older children (10 years of age and older) showed prevalence rates that were more in line with the institutionalized sample (8–12%).

The prevalence estimates from Oliver et al. (1987) are consistent with the 1998 and 1995 British surveys and, importantly, they are also consistent with results from North America. Schroeder et al. (1978), for example, found that 10% of the 1,150 residents in a North Carolina institution had SIB and this figure remained consistent over the three years of the study. When community samples and children are surveyed, lower prevalence rates are reported. This was certainly the case in Texas, where Griffin et al. (1987) surveyed a community sample of 2,663 developmentally disabled children and adolescents and found the prevalence of SIB to be less than 3%. However, it is likely that prevalence estimates from community samples are less accurate because it is more difficult to count the total number of people with developmental disabilities who are out there in the community as opposed to those who live in an institution. Oliver et al. (1987) acknowledged that it was more difficult to estimate the prevalence of SIB for community individuals compared to institutional residents. This is an important point to remember when we review the relation between placement and prevalence in Chapter 2.

What about comparing studies in terms of the topographies of SIB identified? In addition to estimating prevalence, Oliver et al. also recorded the specific forms of SIB among the 596 individuals for whom complete data were available. The resulting list is shown in the left column of Table 1.3. As before, data from the 1995 data from the British survey (Emerson et al., 2001) appear in the right column for comparison purposes. As with aggression, the match is not identical, but still we see what appear to be similar forms of SIB in both studies. Further comparison of Oliver et al. (1987) and Emerson et al. (2001) confirms again that multiple forms were more the rule than the exception. In Oliver et al.'s sample of 596 SIB cases, over half (54%) showed more than one form of SIB. In Emerson et al. the corresponding figure was (72%). As with aggressive behaviors then, we start to see consistency in estimates of the prevalence and forms of SIB among populations of individuals with developmental disabilities, although with both aggression and self-injury there is some tendency for researchers to use different terms to describe what might actually be the same behavior. Teeth banging and teeth grinding, for example, probably refer to the same behavior, although we cannot be sure. Perhaps banging and grinding reflect subtle differences that may or may not be important when it comes to the classification and naming of SIB topographies. In any event, Table 1.3 indicates that there is some variety in the terms used to name the common forms of SIB.

Table 1.3 Comparison of the prevalence of specific forms of self-injurious behavior (SIB) in the Oliver et al. (1987) and Emerson et al. (2001) surveys

Oliver et al. (1987)	Emerson et al. (2001)
Skin picking (39%)	Hits head with hand/body part (47%)
Bites self (38%)	Bites self (45%)
Head punching/slapping (36%)	Hits head with/against objects (42%)
Banging head with or against object (28%)	Hits body with hand/body part (35%)
Hitting body with or against object (10%)	Hits body with/against objects (27%)
Trichotillomania (pulls out hair) (8%)	Pinches/scratches self (19/20%)
Punching/slapping body (7%)	Pica (eats inedible objects) (19%)
Eye poking (6%)	Stuff fingers in body openings (12%)
Pinching self (4%)	Polydipsia (excessive drinking) (11%)
Cutting self with an object (2%)	Trichotillomania (pulls out own hair) (11%)
Poking self in the anus (2%)	Bruxism (teeth grinding) (7%)
Poking self in other locations (2%)	Self-induced vomiting (4%)
Tool banging (2%)	Aerophagia (swallow air) (1%)
Chewing on lips (1%)	Other self-injury (10%)
Nail removal (1%)	
Teeth banging (1%)	
Other self-injury (10%)	

Classification

This variety in terminology highlights a more general lack of consensus on the terms that should be used to name specific topographies of challenging behavior. Sometimes technical terms are brought into service (e.g. trichotillomania); but mainly researchers tend to co-opt existing ordinary terms (e.g. pulling out own hair) to name common forms of challenging behavior. Ordinary terms have the advantage of not only providing a name, but also a readily understood description of the behavior. Still, communication about and understanding of challenging behavior might improve if investigators were to develop at least a more consistent vocabulary for naming the topographies of challenging behavior and in some cases this may require adopting more technical terms.

For now we are stuck with a rather varied vocabulary that complicates classification. This complication does not, however, preclude us from proposing a tentative classification by type and inventory of the commonly reported forms of challenging behavior in people with developmental disabilities. Tables 1.1, 1.2 and 1.3 can be viewed as a beginning classification and inventory. This is only a beginning because the lists of behaviors in these tables, while empirically derived, are neither necessarily complete nor representative and there is by no means full agreement across studies as to the rank ordering of common forms. It is impossible to say with certainty that head banging is more prevalent than self-biting, but we can say that both are common forms of SIB and that SIB itself is consistently found in a significant percentage of people with developmental disabilities.

The inventory must be considered tentative because identical behaviors might be named differently across studies and, alternatively, behaviors with the same or similar names might in fact be quite different. The inventory is also clearly not complete. It omits common forms of stereotyped movements, such as body rocking, head weaving, and hand flapping, which can be challenging (Berkson and Davenport, 1962; Berkson, Rafaeli-Mor and Tarnovsky, 1999). The distinction and relation between stereotyped movements and other major types of challenging behavior is not clear. Any such inventory must therefore be considered tentative because the distinctions between various types or classes of challenging behavior are not always clear. To some, teeth grinding (bruxism) is a stereotyped movement, but others call it self-injury. An inventory of challenging behavior can never be considered complete because it must leave room for topographies that might not now be considered serious, but which could develop into challenging behaviors. Seemingly benign forms of stereotyped movements might develop into serious self-injurious behaviors (Hall, Oliver and Murphy, 2001; Murphy et al., 1999). It must also leave room for unique and idiosyncratic forms of challenging behaviors that are relevant to a few people or perhaps just one person.

Description

An inventory of the common types and forms of challenging behaviors, even one based on good prevalence estimates, is to some extent an abstraction. We cannot even begin to assess and intervene effectively until we move beyond this abstract conceptualization. Moving beyond the abstraction requires a concrete description of the behavior of the individual. That is, a description of the specific acts in the person's repertoire that are considered challenging. For the description to be at all useful it must reference observable behaviors that can be measured accurately. The description must also be valid in the sense that it must cover the actual acts of conduct that are the problem.

We often receive requests from worried parents, teachers, or care staff wanting help with their child's, student's, or client's "behavior." While we typically have some idea of what specific acts might have prompted the request, our first task is always to solicit a more precise description (e.g. "Can you tell me what exactly your child does?"). That is, we are less concerned with getting a name or label and more concerned with getting a good description.

Chamberlain, Chung and Jenner (1993) correctly note that the term "challenging behavior" is descriptive, not diagnostic (p. 118). And yet, while this term might offer some degree of description to those familiar with its usage, calling an act challenging – or aggressive, or self-injurious for that matter – is not sufficiently descriptive for research or clinical purposes. Furthermore, the aim of description is not to describe an individual, but rather to describe the individual's behavior. An individual is not aggressive or self-injurious, but rather the individual engages in aggressive behavior or self-injurious behavior. It is these behaviors of the individual that need to be described in terms of topography, frequency and severity.

It is also important to note that terms such as aggression, self-injury and disruption are to some extent a form of social construction. It is therefore important to ensure that the description of challenging behavior, be it a description of an aggressive, self-injurious or disruptive act, has good construct validity. That is, it should be more or less obvious that the specific behaviors or acts described do in fact constitute a form of aggression or self-injury or disruption, for example.

The literature contains hundreds of descriptions of challenging behaviors in people with developmental disabilities. Some descriptions are better than others of course, but it is not hard to find good examples that can serve as models of the level of specificity that is required for research and clinical practice. Let us consider three examples.

First, James K. Luiselli and his colleagues (Luiselli et al. 2000) described a 12-year old boy named Sam who had autism and was referred for the treatment of his aggressive behaviors. Their description of the child's aggression is a model of comprehensiveness and precision.

> An *Aggressive Episode* was defined as Sam biting, scratching, hitting, pinching, pulling hair, or grabbing the clothing of a student or staff person. Typically, an aggressive episode occurred as several assaultive responses that were displayed while Sam screamed and vocalized loudly. (p. 222)

Now consider this description of self-injurious behavior in an 11-year-old child, Joe, who had developmental and physical disabilities:

> Self-injury was recorded when Joe slapped himself in the face or moved his head so that his forehead or mouth made forceful contact with the floor, table, forearm, or knee. Self-injury typically occurred in discrete, rapid bursts of high intensity. (Sigafoos, Pennell and Versluis, 1996, pp. 104–5)

Our third and final example is a description of challenging behavior that appeared in a 1997 issue of *Mental Retardation*. This description covered several types of behaviors that were shown by two adult men with developmental disabilities:

> Challenging behavior consisted of aggression (e.g., hitting, kicking, or grabbing others), disruption (e.g., throwing, ripping, breaking objects, and yelling), or stereotyped movements, such as body-rocking, hand-flapping, spitting, or head-weaving. (Sigafoos et al., 1997, p. 201).

Additional examples could be provided, but these three are sufficient to illustrate the major elements of a good initial description – or definition really – for research and clinical purposes. Fundamental to a good description is a focus on observable behavior. Luiselli et al. (2000) talked about biting, scratching, hitting, pinching, pulling hair and grabbing clothing. Sigafoos et al. (1996) referred to face slapping and head banging and Sigafoos et al. (1997) listed specific and observable forms of challenging behaviors (e.g. hitting, kicking, breaking objects, body-rocking and hand-flapping).

The idea is that the challenging behavior must be described in such a way as to make it accessible to an observer. An observer could see a person hitting someone else, see a person banging their head on their knee, and see someone ripping out the pages of a book or flapping her hands. Screaming and yelling of course might not be observed, but such behaviors can be heard and recorded, which makes them accessible to an observer.

This emphasis on observable acts of conduct is quite different from talking about anger, frustration, rage or other emotional states, which figure heavily in some theories of challenging behavior. This is not to say that an individual's emotional state is not relevant to, or has no connection to, observable behavior. Rather this emphasis is based on the assumption that it is the observable behavior that is "the problem." It is a good assumption. A child might be referred for uncontrollable anger or temper tantrums, but when a more specific description of the problem is solicited, the concern typically boils down to something that can be observed. A treatment that did not lead to clinically significant reductions in the overt acts of hitting, kicking and pinching others, for example, would not be considered successful. This emphasis also directs treatment to its rightful target, which is to reduce the frequency and severity of challenging behavior.

In addition to working up a good description focused on observable behaviors, a related activity is developing a measurement and recording system that is accurate (reliable) and captures the nature of the typical episode (valid). A clinician might arbitrarily decide to count each time a child hits another person. On the face of it this would seem to be a sensible approach. With a good definition in hand, this approach might even yield highly accurate and reliable data. That is, it might prove easy to count each and every instance of the behavior and the recordings of two independent observers might prove to be highly consistent (i.e. reliable). However, this would not be a good approach if the child's typical episode involved not only trying to hit others, but also trying to kick, pinch and pull their hair. In this case, recording only the number of times the child hit the other person would seem to miss much that is important, to say the least. The measurement and recording system must therefore conform to the previously developed description, rather than the other way around.

Research and clinical practice both require an initial and good description of the dependent variable, which for our purposes is the pattern of challenging behavior shown by the individual. A measurement system is then designed that will best enable the described behavioral pattern to be recorded accurately. A good description can never be obtained merely by asking another person, no matter how well that person might know the client. This is a useful first step of course, but developing a useful description that can later be linked to an appropriate measurement system will also require careful observation of the individual's behavior.

With a good initial description of the pattern of challenging behavior shown by the individual, it is easy to develop an appropriate measurement system; without a good initial description it is impossible. Implementing an appropriate measurement system is the next step in the descriptive process. The idea here is to obtain a representative sample of the behavior so as to estimate the frequency and severity of the described pattern of behavior. This requires repeated measures of the behavior throughout the day and across a number of days, activities and conditions. This requirement is similar to what others might think of as obtaining a baseline of the behavior. In most intervention research, however, baseline observations (and intervention observations for that matter) are typically limited to brief (10 minute) sessions, conducted over a number of days to be sure, but most often confined to a specific time and activity during the day (Didden, Duker and Korzilius, 1997). It is unclear therefore if the baselines obtained in the typical intervention study provide a truly representative sample of the individual's pattern of challenging behavior. Additional assessments prior to baseline are therefore of potential value in not only helping one formulate a good description, but also in ensuring one obtains a more representative sample of challenging behavior (see Chapter 6).

There are of course practical constraints that make it difficult to collect more comprehensive samples of behaviors in the context of intervention research, but it has been accomplished in several studies. Luiselli et al. (2000), for example, recorded how many *Aggressive Episodes* occurred each day and throughout the day. They continued recording Sam's behavior in this way over a number of days. From this they were able to show that Sam had on average 2–5 episodes each day. They also designed a system for recording the intensity of Sam's behaviors, which involved recording when the episode was so severe that it required the use of emergency intervention (i.e. time-out, protective holding). Sigafoos et al. (1996) collected brief (5-minute) videotapes of Joe over three days, but did so across the six major activities that comprised his entire school day. These videotapes were then scored to determine the percentage of intervals with SIB in each of the six major activities. From this, the researchers discovered that Joe engaged in almost constant self-injury during periods of low stimulation and almost no self-injury during times when he was involved in an activity.

As you might now appreciate, this type of data is essential to gaining a better picture or description of the pattern of an individual's challenging behavior. In many cases, the frequency and severity of challenging behavior will conform to a predictable and describable pattern. Once described, this pattern can help to explain the behavior and, in turn, point to appropriate treatment approaches.

Description then is the first step along the road to explaining and treating challenging behavior. It is a step that must be individualized to ensure the description captures the behavioral patterns at the level of the individual. There could thus be as many descriptions of challenging behavior as there are individuals with challenging behavior. While this is true in one sense, there would be little point in studying this thing called challenging behavior if there were not some generalizations that could be gained from pooling individual descriptions. Each of our three examples provided at the beginning of this section is a description of challenging behavior at the individual level, and yet you might have noticed how each is in fact consistent with some of the general findings from the prevalence studies in the types (i.e. aggression, self-injury, property destruction) and multiple forms of challenging behaviors identified.

Unlike the image that might be formed from the prevalence studies, however, challenging behavior does not often seem to occur as a specific discrete behavior. While a person might be identified in a prevalence study as engaging in aggression and the form of the aggression might be listed as hitting and kicking others, a more detailed description is likely to show that the behavior occurs in a burst of responding that might be better conceptualized as an episode of aggressive acts rather than as a single discrete act taking a specific form. Consider another typical example. A child's tantrum might last 10–20 minutes and it might include various forms of challenging behavior, such as screaming, crying, aggression, property destruction and self-injury. In a prevalence study, this might be reported as a tantrum or as disruption, aggression, property destruction, and self-injury. If the only time self-injury occurred was when the child was also screaming, aggressing and destroying property, then it may in fact be better to think of this pattern as a cluster of behaviors (i.e. as a tantrum) that included a number of more specific forms.

This raises a final issue that should be considered when it comes to describing challenging behavior at the level of the individual. The description must fit the pattern of behavior and the pattern of behavior is likely to change from episode to episode. Consider again the tantrum. You observe a tantrum by a young autistic boy that involves crying and thrashing about on the floor. Your definition of a tantrum might thus be "any time the child falls to floor and cries for more than 30 seconds." In a subsequent tantrum, however, the child wanders around the room crying and slapping himself in the face. This does not meet your definition of a tantrum, but functionally it could be useful to conceptualize it as the same type of episode. The definition of what constitutes an instance of challenging behavior must therefore be loose enough to consider the range of topographies that might occur in varying combinations within and across episodes as well as the minor variations that are likely to be observed in any given topography. A description that is too precise or too exact may exclude minor variations or new topographies that are really part of the same response class. This means that the initial description must often be revised in light of any changes to the individual's pattern of challenging behavior. Description is not only a necessary first step, but it is also an ongoing step in the understanding, explanation, assessment and treatment of challenging behavior.

Summary and conclusion

Developmental disability is an umbrella term that covers a variety of conditions, but all of these conditions affect learning, development and behavior in significant ways, and no doubt also affect the emergence and persistence of challenging behavior. Although terminology and definitions are contentious and vary, there is an emerging consensus as to the type and forms of behavior that are considered challenging in individuals with developmental disabilities. When these major types and forms are considered, challenging behaviors are estimated to occur in approximately 15–17% of individuals with developmental disabilities. The overall results from prevalence surveys lead us to the conclusion that there is a consistently identified set of challenging behaviors that can be classified into a few major types and which are highly prevalent in people with developmental disabilities. Once an individual is identified as having challenging behavior, a next step is to develop an objective description of the problem. Only when the pattern of challenging behavior has been comprehensively described can the task of explanation begin.

Chapter 2

Risk factors for challenging behavior

Introduction

In this chapter we review factors that appear to place the individual at increased risk for challenging behavior. A review of risk factors will set the stage and facilitate our attempt to explain why there is such a high prevalence of challenging behavior in people with developmental disabilities. The explanation begun here will be more fully developed into the systematic account or theory of challenging behavior that is developed in Chapter 3. The explanation that we offer is focused on a consideration of risk factors that seem to contribute to the emergence and maintenance of challenging behavior. We do not assume that this approach to explanation will necessarily account for all challenging behavior in all individuals with developmental disabilities. However, if these factors should also by chance correspond to important characteristics that distinguish people with developmental disabilities from the general population, then this may help to explain the higher prevalence of challenging behavior in people with developmental disabilities when compared with people without disabilities, and more specifically, why some individuals with developmental disabilities have challenging behaviors, but others do not. If our explanations have any merit whatsoever, they should also point to useful approaches to assessment and intervention. In addition, effective assessments and interventions should be consistent with the explanation.

Any attempt to explain challenging behavior must be able to account for the fact that, while challenging behaviors are prevalent in populations of people with developmental disabilities, not everyone with a developmental disability shows challenging behavior. In fact, the majority of people surveyed in the prevalence studies are not identified as having challenging behavior. Challenging behavior cannot therefore be attributed simply to the fact that the person has a developmental disability. Something else must account for why a significant percentage of people with developmental disabilities have challenging behavior, but most others do not.

Risk factors

One way to begin this account is to think in terms of risk factors. Here it will help to recall two important points from Chapter 1. First, developmental disabilities are heterogeneous and individuals with developmental disabilities will present with varying characteristics and varying degrees of disability. Second, there is a range of prevalence estimates for challenging behavior when you compare results across studies on different samples or subpopulations.

In Chapter 1 we hinted at the possibility that these differing prevalence estimates might arise from the fact that the individuals surveyed in one study differ on average and in some important way from individuals surveyed in another study. When prevalence figures differ across studies, it could be because the individuals in these studies differ. Suppose the prevalence of SIB is estimated at 15% in one study and 3% in another. Now, suppose that the 3% estimate came from a sample of people with mild/moderate mental retardation, whereas the 15% estimate came from a sample of people with severe/profound mental retardation. If this general trend proved to be consistent both within and across a good number of studies, which it is by the way, then severity of mental retardation could be viewed as a risk factor for SIB.

Many prevalence studies have identified individual characteristics that are consistently associated with a higher prevalence of challenging behavior. That is, within a population or sample of people with developmental disabilities, a greater percentage of those who share these characteristics to a similar extent will be identified as having challenging behavior when compared to individuals who do not share these characteristics to the same degree. Those characteristics consistently associated with an increased prevalence of challenging behavior are rightly conceptualized as potential "risk factors." Our intention is to first direct your attention to each of the major potential risk factors and then weave these into a theory of challenging behavior in Chapter 3 that will hopefully help to explain why and how some of these factors place the individual at risk for challenging behavior.

Severity of intellectual disability

In an important update on a 1979 book chapter, a team lead by Stephen R. Schroeder from the University of Kansas could write with confidence that "the prevalence of SIB, aggression, and property destruction increases with severity of mental retardation" (Schroeder et al., 1997, p. 444). Schroeder et al. (1997) also noted, however, that the details of this inverse relation between prevalence of challenging behavior and intellectual functioning are a bit more complicated than the above quote would first lead you to believe. While a higher percentage of individuals with severe mental retardation will generally be identified with challenging behavior, when compared with individuals with mild/moderate mental retardation, this trend does not hold for people with multiple/profound disabilities. That is, people with profound mental retardation are not necessarily at any greater risk for challenging behavior in comparison with people with severe mental retardation and this is not due to a ceiling effect. Instead it is most probably related to the fact that many people with profound mental retardation have associated conditions, such as physical impairment, which simply makes it difficult or impossible for them to perform many of the most common topographies of challenging behavior.

Neither does this general relation hold for certain specific topographies of challenging behavior. Verbal aggression is more prevalent among people with mild/moderate disabilities, most obviously because people with more severe disabilities typically lack any appreciable amount of speech. This may account for Emerson et al.'s (2001) finding that aggression was more prevalent among those who were "higher functioning" given that verbal aggression was the second most commonly identified topography of aggression in their study. In 1992, the Australian psychiatrist Stewart Einfeld also found that the type of challenging behavior in individuals with developmental disabilities differed with their level of IQ. Specifically, aggression and property destruction were the more typical types of challenging behavior in people with IQ scores in the mild to moderate range of mental retardation, whereas self-injury and stereotyped behaviors were more frequently identified in persons with IQ scores in the severe range of mental retardation. Consistent with the general shape of the relation summarized by Schroeder et al. (1997), Einfeld also found that ratings of challenging behavior tended to decline for individuals who had profound levels of intellectual disability when compared with the ratings for individuals with severe mental retardation.

In considering this relation, it is important to bear in mind that severity of disability is typically scaled in terms of intellectual functioning as determined by an IQ test, but severity of intellectual disability is not independent of adaptive behavior functioning (Luckasson et al., 1992). Lower IQ scores are associated with more substantial deficits in adaptive behavior functioning. In addition, associated conditions, such as seizure disorders, physical impairments and identifiable organic syndromes become more common as severity of intellectual disability increases (Graziano, 2002). Therefore, the higher prevalence of challenging behavior in people with more severe mental retardation is not necessarily attributable solely to lower IQ.

In addition, the nature of intelligence and its relation to IQ testing is controversial (Fraser, 1995; Herrnstein and Murray, 1994). Still, IQ tests do seem to do one thing fairly well and that is to predict educational achievement, which must have something to do with intelligence and learning. Some individuals, given similar educational experiences, appear more intelligent than others in that they learn more and learn more quickly. Individuals with higher IQs might therefore be expected to acquire more adaptive behaviors and acquire these more quickly and easily than individuals with comparatively lower IQs because adaptive behaviors are for the most part learned behaviors. Some such differences in the learning of adaptive behaviors are no doubt related to numerous variables, such as motivational factors, the quality of instruction received, physical limitations and the individual's health and home life, for example. Still, it is not unreasonable to assume that individual differences in the extent and speed of learning (and the ease of teaching for that matter) might influence the emergence and persistence of adaptive behaviors, which in turn might influence the emergence and persistence of challenging behavior (see Chapter 3).

The degree of intellectual disability, as measured by an IQ test, might therefore predict to some extent, and determine either directly or indirectly, how much and how quickly a person learns and, correspondingly, how easy it is to teach that person. As we show later (Chapter 3), learning assumes a significant role in our theory of challenging behavior. For now, we simply note that the evidence from numerous prevalence studies reveals a consistent relation between severity of intellectual disability and prevalence of challenging behavior. Any explanation of challenging behavior must therefore incorporate and account for this fact.

Type of disability

In addition to severity, there are some fairly well established relations between certain types of developmental disorders or syndromes and the prevalence of challenging behavior. These relations might be viewed as biological risk factors. Individuals with severe autism, for example, tend to have among the highest prevalence of challenging behavior of all the major developmental disability types (Sturmey and Vernon, 2001; Wing and Attwood, 1987). In addition, certain forms of challenging behavior are closely associated with specific syndromes. Some of the most apparent syndrome–behavior relations include the high prevalence of SIB in

persons with Lesch-Nyhan (Lesch and Nyhan, 1964) and Cornelia de
Lange syndromes (Cataldo and Harris, 1982). In addition, stereotyped
hand mannerisms, which can cause injury, are a ubiquitous and defining
feature of Rett Syndrome (Olson and Rett, 1985). There also appears to
be a high prevalence of SIB and aggression in individuals with Prader-Willi
Syndrome (Symons et al., 1999). These links are intriguing and suggest
that biological factors must be considered in any systematic account of
challenging behavior.

Knowledge of biological risk factors for challenging behavior is changing rapidly as more and more syndrome–behavior relations or behavioral
phenotypes are identified (Gillberg and O'Brien, 2000). Even with these
advances, however, it is important to point out that the diagnosis for certain conditions and syndromes remains less than perfect, especially for
conditions such as autism for which there are currently no biological
markers. In addition, not all individuals who are considered at risk for
challenging behavior, because of some biological condition such as
Cornelia de Lange syndrome for example, have challenging behavior.
Furthermore, not all individuals with developmental disabilities and challenging behaviors have a specific identified syndrome or specific
biological risk factor.

All of these caveats should be setting off alarm bells for those who
might have expected biology to fully explain challenging behavior.
Biology is clearly part of the story, but is by no means the whole story.
Still, any account of challenging behavior will need to explain how and
why some biological factors or conditions appear to increase the risk of
challenging behavior, but do not precisely nor fully determine whether or
not any given individual will be identified as having challenging behavior.
A better way to frame the issue then is not to ask whether biological factors cause challenging behavior, but rather to ask how biological factors
interact with social and environmental variables to shape and maintain
challenging behavior. The explanation that we will outline more fully in
Chapter 3 encompasses mechanisms that show how biological factors
could interact with environmental and learning factors in ways that would
lead to the emergence and maintenance of challenging behavior.

Gender

Gender does not appear to be a major risk factor for challenging behavior.

In the British survey (Emerson et al., 2001; Kiernan and Qureshi,
1993), a higher percentage of those identified with challenging behavior
were males (65–58%). However, this difference is difficult to interpret
without knowing the proportion of males to females in the overall population of individuals with developmental disabilities. In addition, the
differences in the percentage of males and females identified as having

challenging behavior in the 1998 British survey were not statistically significant for any major type of challenging behavior in the 1988 survey. In the smaller 1995 survey, however, males were significantly more common among those with destructive behaviors. This suggests that in some samples there may be some gender differences in the types and forms of challenging behaviors that are most prevalent. Aggressive behavior, for example, appears to be more common in males, whereas there appear to be no such gender differences for SIB (Schroeder et al., 1997, p. 444), although there may be some gender differences in the prevalence of various topographies of SIB. Oliver et al. (1987), for example, found that females were more likely to pull out their own hair, whereas males were more likely to hit their body with an object.

Gender may therefore be relevant to the type and form of challenging behavior that is likely to emerge. One could speculate as to why this might be true. Perhaps females are more likely to show self-injurious hair pulling because they generally have longer hair or because caregivers put more emphasis on female hair care. Aggressive and destructive behaviors might be more common in males because men tend to be bigger and stronger than women and they might therefore have less to fear by way of retaliation from their victims. All of this is highly speculative, however, and it is unclear if the female with challenging behavior is really much different from her male counterpart.

It is important to remember that a significant percentage of individuals with developmental disabilities have challenging behaviors and this significant percentage includes both males and females in relatively close, but not identical, proportions. Whatever mechanisms account for this high prevalence must therefore affect both males and females, although perhaps in ways that differentially select certain types and forms of behaviors in males more so than in females and vice versa.

Age

Challenging behaviors can begin within the first six months of life, but in most cases these behaviors tend to emerge at 2–3 years of age (Schroeder et al., 1997). After emerging in the preschool years, the 1988 and 1995 British data showed that the prevalence of challenging behaviors tends to increase throughout childhood and adolescence (Emerson et al., 2001; Kiernan and Qureshi, 1993). After this developmental period, however, the prevalence of challenging behavior tends to level off and actually begins to decline. This decline becomes most noticeable at two different times based on severity of disability. For individuals with severe mental retardation the decline begins at age 50, whereas for those with less severe disabilities the decline begins at 19 years of age.

In considering how age might influence challenging behavior it is useful to consider what is happening at the time of the major milestones in the prevalence trend line. That is, what is happening to the person during those periods of time that mark the emergence (2–3 years), increase (3–18 years) and subsequent decline in the prevalence of challenging behavior (19 or 50 years of age). Of course these events or milestones may be substantially delayed, substantially different, or never in fact realized for some individuals because of the nature and severity of their developmental disability. Still, let us consider the major changes that might be expected at each of these developmental periods.

The initial emergence of challenging behavior at around 2–3 years of age corresponds to a time when gross and fine motor skills become more coordinated and fluent (Graziano, 2002). Challenging behaviors may become more prevalent at this time simply because the topographies of hitting or kicking or throwing objects enter the repertoire of possible response options. With this emerging fluency in motor skills also comes increased strength, meaning that any existing or emerging acts of aggression, self-injury or property destruction can now start to cause noticeable injury and damage and are therefore more likely to attract the attention and concern of caregivers.

The increasing prevalence of challenging behaviors through adolescence corresponds to the years of schooling during which various demands are made of the child, peer relations become increasing important, and of course major maturational changes occur. At 19 years of age, formal schooling ends and so too might some of the maturational changes associated with adolescence. For those with mild and moderate intellectual disabilities, one might expect further development of a sense of maturity which could make challenging behavior a less attractive option and one that is now subject to greater negative consequences (e.g. losing a job rather than merely suffering a period of time-out at school). The lifestyle and responsibilities for persons with more severe disabilities, in contrast, may not change very much after the school years. Many of these individuals are likely to continue to have restricted lifestyles and participate in day programs that involve similar demands to those experienced during the school years. After 50 years of age, the requirement to participate in day and vocational programs may cease. At this time, it is also important to recognize the more general effects of ageing (reduced vision, hearing and mobility), all of which would seem to reduce general levels of activity, including challenging behavior. The age trends in the prevalence of challenging behavior might therefore be explained by considering how developmental changes might alter a person's physical capabilities and how environmental changes affect the person's lifestyle and the expectations made of the person.

Adaptive behavior functioning

One of the characteristics that distinguish people with developmental disability from those without it is that the former have obvious and substantial deficits in several areas of adaptive behavior functioning. Adaptive behaviors refer to the skills that are necessary to participate in the major activities of daily life (Luckasson et al., 1992). Adaptive behaviors, such as dressing, greeting others and purchasing items at a store, are typically grouped into one of several domains. Some of the major domains common to many standardized measures of adaptive behavior include self-care, motor, communication, social, academic, vocational, and community living domains.

Although adaptive behavior functioning can be difficult to assess, it is generally the case that the extent of deficit in adaptive behavior functioning is one indication of the severity of the person's developmental disability. Individuals who are unable to feed and dress themselves, wash and toilet themselves, speak, make choices and more generally indicate their wants and needs are likely to be labeled as having a severe to profound degree of developmental disability. Individuals who, on the other hand, have learned to feed, dress, and toilet themselves, but not to initiate and maintain social interactions, follow spoken directions, read or write, seek or maintain employment are perhaps more likely to be described as having a mild or moderate disability.

In some cases, the reason for the deficit or lack of a particular skill may be related to physical impairment. A child who cannot move her legs or arms very well because of cerebral palsy, for example, might never be able to walk independently or move a spoon full of food to her mouth in the normal way. In such cases, the deficit is not a learning issue, but rather a physical capability issue. It is true then that physical reasons often underlie the deficits in adaptive behavior functioning that are evident in some individuals with developmental disabilities. In other cases, however, the deficits do not appear to be related to physical incapacity, but rather appear to stem from impairment of learning. That is, for some reason the individual has not acquired the adaptive behaviors that would be typical for a person of that age in that culture.

Why is it that individuals with developmental disabilities, even when they have the physical capability to do so, never learn the range of adaptive skills that others seem to learn so early and easily? One factor might be related to learning impairment. Adaptive behaviors represent learned behaviors. If there is a deficit in adaptive behavior that cannot be attributed to lack of physical capability, then it might be useful to look at why the behavior has not been learnt. Perhaps there is impairment of learning ability or weakness in the teaching approach, or both.

In an important paper published in 1996, Bob Remington from the University of Southampton outlined the basic learning processes that can be used in teaching people with developmental disabilities. The basic learning processes Remington outlined included respondent and operant conditioning procedures, as well as what might be thought of as more symbolic or more advanced social learning processes. Individuals with developmental disabilities have difficulty with learning in general, but they appear to experience particular difficulties learning via the more social and symbolic processes. The difficulties faced in trying to teach adaptive skills to individuals with developmental disabilities could therefore stem in part from heavy reliance on teaching strategies that are based on social and symbolic learning processes, such as incidental teaching, verbal instruction, modeling and observational learning. The rather incidental, almost accidental, way in which the typically developing child learns basic self-care, play, social and communication skills is generally neither sufficient nor very effective for the individual with a developmental disability. Thus in the absence of well-designed teaching programs that incorporate principles of respondent and operant conditioning, the individual may fail to show much gain in adaptive behavior functioning over time even though they may be exposed to developmental experiences which are similar to those of non-handicapped children. As we noted in the previous section of this chapter on the "Severity of intellectual disability," deficits in adaptive behavior may be related to impairment of certain learning processes and this impairment of learning may in turn help to explain the emergence and maintenance of challenging behavior.

The point of this rather extended consideration of adaptive behavior is to remind readers that many of the most basic skills of daily life are often either completely absent or so poorly developed in people with developmental disabilities that they often do not function with any meaningful degree of independence in several important domains of daily living. As we made clear in Chapter 1, everyone with a developmental disability will by definition have significant deficits in some areas of adaptive behavior functioning. The issue then is whether the degree or severity of the deficit and the precise skills or domains affected have some specific relation to the prevalence of challenging behavior.

Evidence from the prevalence studies overall suggests that deficits in certain specific adaptive skill domains are associated with an increased risk of challenging behavior. In particular deficits in the self-care (e.g. eating, dressing, washing, toileting), gross motor (e.g. mobility), and communication (e.g. receptive and expressive speech) domains appear to increase the risk of challenging behavior (Borthwick-Duffy, 1994; Emerson et al., 2001; Kiernan and Qureshi, 1993; Schroeder et al., 1997). Analysis of the British survey data from both 1988 and 1995, for example, indicated that challenging behavior was more severe for those who had greater need for assistance with eating, dressing, and washing and among those who had greater deficits in receptive and expressive language (Emerson et al., 2001, p. 88).

Other studies have reported similar associations, especially for the link between communication deficits and challenging behavior. Schroeder et al. (1978), for example, found that individuals identified as having SIB had significantly greater receptive and expressive language impairment in comparison with individuals from the same institution who did not have SIB. Similar findings for challenging behavior in general have been reported by others including Chamberlain et al. (1993). The hypothesis that deficits in the speech/language domain may be a uniquely important risk factor for challenging behavior (Beitchman and Peterson, 1986) is based in part on such findings.

Deficits in the social skills domain have also been isolated as a potentially unique contributor to challenging behavior in persons with developmental disabilities. The potential link between social skills and challenging behavior has been most thoroughly investigated by Johnny Matson and his colleagues at Louisiana State University in Baton Rouge (Matson, Anderson and Bamburg, 2000; Matson, Smiroldo and Bamburg, 1998). In one of a series of studies, the LSU team assessed social skills in four groups of individuals with developmental disabilities (Duncan et al., 1999). One group was made up of individuals with self-injury, another of individuals with aggression, a third had both behaviors, and the fourth group consisted of individuals who did not have any challenging behavior. They found a restricted range of social skills among the three groups of individuals with challenging behavior as compared with the fourth control group. In addition, individuals with self-injury tended to have a different social skills profile to individuals with aggression. These data suggest that deficits in social skills in general, and deficits in certain specific patterns of social skills, may be related to an increased risk of self-injury or aggression.

In considering what this relation might mean, it is important to consider the possibility that the construct of social skills may not necessarily be completely independent of other areas of adaptive behavior functioning. Much of course will depend on how social skills are defined and measured and these vary from study to study. The social skills domain may therefore overlap with other areas of adaptive behavior functioning. It is the case, for instance, that the expression of certain skills considered to represent the social skills domain (e.g. initiating conversations, complimenting others, saying thank you), appears also to require a rather high level of speech and language skills. Therefore, individuals with developmental disability who lack speech would also be expected to have major deficits in social skills.

And so, while the associations between deficits in certain areas of adaptive behavior functioning and increased frequency or severity of challenging behavior could very well be pointing to uniquely important risk factors for challenging behavior, we find that it is exceedingly difficult to draw firm conclusions on the unique importance of any specific area of adaptive behavior. One reason for this difficulty is that the measures used to assess adaptive behaviors in the prevalence studies are often less than comprehensive. That is, in many of the prevalence studies, the assessment of an individual's skills in any given area of adaptive behavior functioning, say language for example, is typically limited to a relatively small number of items or questions, which might therefore provide a rather gross estimate of the person's abilities in that domain. More comprehensive assessments would likely provide a better profile of an individual's adaptive behavior deficits across several domains. The luxury of in-depth and individualized adaptive behavior assessments is, however, rarely obtainable in a large prevalence study because of the time and cost.

A second difficulty stems from the fact that deficits in one area of adaptive behavior functioning tend to go hand in hand with deficits in other areas (McGrew and Bruininks, 1989). Individuals with developmental disabilities who have severely impaired speech and language, for example, also tend to have severe deficits in other adaptive skills such as self-care, leisure and social skills (Sigafoos and Pennell, 1995). This trend is especially marked in individuals with severe disabilities, who also tend to have the highest prevalence of challenging behavior.

Given these difficulties, the critical question as to whether a deficit in one domain, say speech and language development or social skills, is a risk factor for challenging behavior over and above deficits in the other areas of adaptive behavior probably cannot be resolved in prevalence studies alone. Despite these difficulties, our reading of the available evidence leads us to the tentative conclusion that deficits in certain areas of adaptive behavior functioning do seem to increase the risk of challenging behavior. These areas are speech/language, self-care, gross motor, and the social skills domain. But this tentative conclusion should not be taken to mean that any of these areas of deficit are directly or causally related to a higher prevalence of challenging behavior. Such could be the case, but for now we must take a more cautious approach to interpreting these relations. The relation between deficits in certain areas of adaptive behavior functioning and challenging behavior could instead reflect the effects of more general impairments in development and learning, as we shall see.

Substantial deficits in the areas we have just outlined – speech/language, self-care, gross motor, and social skills – are characteristic of more severe levels of mental retardation. Two additional facts bear repeating. First, individuals with more severe disability have the highest prevalence of challenging behavior and second, the relation between adaptive behavior deficits and challenging behavior is not linear. At some point, deficits in adaptive behavior may be so great that certain forms of challenging behavior are precluded, which nicely explains the lower prevalence of challenging behavior in people with profound/multiple disability as revealed in the research of Einfeld (1992) and Schroeder et al. (1997).

Although we are speculating perhaps too much here, it strikes us that the areas of adaptive behavior functioning outlined above (e.g. speech/language, self-care, gross motor, and social skills), consist of skills that typically developing children seem to acquire incidentally without any explicit, deliberate, formal, or systematic instruction and they acquire these skills before enrollment in formal schooling. In fact, typical children seem to readily acquire such skills through nothing more intensive than a bit of verbal instruction, modeling and demonstration; the show and tell method if you will. The fact that these skills are not readily acquired to the same degree by people with developmental disabilities not only distinguishes people with developmental disabilities from those without, but also no doubt reflects deficits in learning amongst the developmentally disabled when teaching is based on more incidental and symbolic processes. What ends up in the person's repertoire, be it adaptive or maladaptive, reflects what the person is capable of physically as well as what the person has learnt. When symbolic learning is severely impaired, skills taught incidentally may never be acquired.

Sensory impairment

Recall from Chapter 1 that developmental disability is an umbrella term covering a number of more specific conditions, such as mental retardation and autism. It is also an umbrella term in the sense that these specific conditions are often associated with other complications, such as physical and sensory impairments. We have already seen how a physical impairment might preclude certain forms or topographies of challenging behavior and there is evidence that vision and hearing impairment may also influence the prevalence and form of challenging behavior, but not necessarily in the same way as a physical impairment.

Since at least 1978 it has been reported that vision and hearing impairment are apparent risk factors for challenging behavior among individuals with developmental disability (Schroeder et al., 1997). We first consider vision impairment. People with developmental disability and vision impairment do seem on average to have a relatively higher prevalence of challenging behavior even for the developmental disability population (Sharma, Sigafoos and Carroll, 2002; Van Hasselt, Kazdin and Hersen,

1986). And, in terms of the topography of challenging behavior, there appear to be certain forms of challenging behavior (e.g. self-injurious eye poking) that are often seen in individuals with visual defects (Bak, 1999). There is also a peculiar class of stereotyped mannerisms, known as blindisms (e.g. rocking, spinning, twitching thumbs, rolling of the eyes up and back into the head), which are common in blind children (Abang, 1985). In a study that offers some confirmation that visual impairment is a risk factor for challenging behavior, Bak (1999) found a high correlation between degree of visual impairment and inappropriate behavior in 202 children with visual impairment. Simply put, children with more restricted vision showed an increased prevalence of unusual and inappropriate behaviors than did children with less severe vision impairment.

Additional confirmation can be found in an analysis of some of the British survey data from both 1988 and 1995 (Emerson et al., 2001). From these analyses there was found to be a statistically significant, but rather low, correlation (0.103) between vision impairment and aggression. It is of potential relevance to note that this analysis did not examine the effect of degree of vision impairment on challenging behavior, which Bak's (1999) study showed to be important. It is therefore possible that higher correlations might have been found for individuals with severe versus more mild or moderate degrees of visual impairment.

Let us now consider the relation between challenging behavior and hearing impairment. There is plenty of evidence pointing to an increased prevalence of challenging behavior among deaf children when deaf children are compared with hearing children (Meadow and Schlesinger, 1971; Mitchell and Quittner, 1996; Schnittjer and Hirshoren, 1981; van Eldik, 1994; van Eldik et al., 2000; Vostanis et al., 1997). This evidence suggests that hearing impairment is indeed a risk factor for challenging behavior, but the extent to which the presence of an associated impairment of hearing increases the risk of challenging behavior among individuals with developmental disabilities could of course be another matter. Turning again to Emerson et al.'s (2001) analyses of the British survey data, one finds that the correlation between hearing impairment and increased prevalence of challenging behavior is very low and certainly not statistically significant for any of the major types of challenging behaviors (i.e. aggression, self-injury, destructive behavior, non-compliance). It is important to point out that, as with vision impairment, the degree of hearing impairment was not factored into this analysis. This could account for the lack of significant correlation in the Emerson et al. report. If hearing impairment were correlated with challenging behavior then one might expect that the correlation would become stronger and approach statistical significance for individuals with more severe hearing impairment as compared with individuals with mild or moderate hearing loss.

That a sensory impairment could be a risk factor for challenging behaviors among individuals with developmental disability is consistent with our emerging view that it is reasonable to look at some risk factors – especially severity of disability and adaptive behavior deficits – in terms of a more general impairment of learning. An individual with developmental disability and an associated vision or hearing impairment would be expected to experience even greater impairment of learning than their severity of intellectual disability would predict given that so much learning and teaching is processed through auditory and visual channels.

Health and medical problems

As is true for everyone, people with developmental disabilities will experience a range of health and medical problems throughout their lives. In fact, and unfortunately, medical researchers have discovered that individuals with developmental disabilities tend to experience even greater health and medical problems than their non-disabled peers (Evenhuis et al., 2001; Lennox, Diggens and Ugoni, 2000). This includes an increased prevalence of psychopathologies such as anxiety disorders, depression, phobia and schizophrenia (Tonge and Einfeld, 1991). The issue to be considered here is not whether such problems occur or even whether such problems occur more frequently in people with developmental disabilities (see Chapter 5), but rather whether there are any specific health and medical problems that increase the risk of challenging behavior. Along these lines, various health and medical problems have been implicated. The primary suspects appear to be seizure disorders (Gedye, 1989), psychiatric disorders (Matson and Barrett, 1993), pains, infections, illnesses (Gunsett et al., 1989), and sleep disturbance (Didden and Sigafoos, 2001).

Helen Beange (1987) stressed the importance of proactive care to maintain health and ensure timely diagnosis and treatment of medical problems in people with developmental disabilities. Health promotion is certainly of critical importance in its own right, but the possibility that unrecognized and untreated health and medical problems may also influence challenging behavior is sufficiently compelling to warrant our advocating a prior and thorough medical screening as part of any attempt to address challenging behavior (see Chapter 5). For now we are focused on whether such conditions represent risk factors for challenging behavior in individuals with developmental disabilities and if so, why and how?

The influence of health and medical problems on challenging behavior in individuals with developmental disabilities has not been studied to any great depth, although some areas, such as the influence of psychopathology, are starting to receive increased attention. Even in the relatively few studies where such connections have been discovered, the nature of the relation is not obvious. Schroeder et al. (1978), for example, found that people with severe SIB were more likely to have a seizure disorder than were individuals who had either mild or no SIB. The difference between the groups was huge. Forty-one percent of those with severe SIB also had a seizure disorder, but only 20–22% of those with mild or no SIB had seizures. Aggression has also been linked to seizure disorders. Gedye (1989), for example, believes that frontal lobe seizures can trigger aggressive outbursts, whereas Woermann and his colleagues (2000) reported that aggressive outbursts were more common among people with temporal lobe epilepsy than among people who did not have epilepsy.

Now it is possible that seizures could directly trigger some forms of challenging behavior, but there are other possibilities that bear consideration. It is not inconceivable, for instance, that repeated and forceful head banging and head hitting – the severe SIB group in the Schroeder et al. (1978) study – could cause serious head trauma that could in turn cause seizures (Graziano, 2002). Thus one could legitimately ask whether seizure disorders increase the risk of self-injury or whether self-injury increases the risk of seizures. Similarly with aggression, one could question whether aggression is a manifestation of certain types of seizures (frontal lobe or temporal lobe?) or whether a seizure, causing pain, makes the person more irritable, which in turn makes him or her more likely to react to even minor annoyances with aggression. The issue of whether seizure disorders are a risk factor for challenging behavior is further complicated by data showing similar patterns of problem behaviors for developmentally disabled individuals with and without an associated seizure disorder (Matson et al., 1999).

An equally complicated issue is the relation between psychopathology and challenging behavior. While individuals with developmental disabilities can certainly have psychiatric disorders, the diagnosis of psychopathology in this population is fraught with problems. Part of the diagnostic quandary stems from the possibility that schizophrenia, depression, and anxiety may manifest in different ways for people with and without developmental disability (Einfeld and Aman, 1995) and the presence of challenging behavior looms large as a basis for making a psychiatric diagnosis in the first place. It is not naïve to ask whether the challenging behavior is a symptom of a psychiatric disorder or whether the diagnosis of a psychiatric disorder is simply more likely to be applied to individuals with challenging behavior.

It is unclear to what extent psychiatric disorders directly cause challenging behavior, but it is becoming clear that in many cases, challenging behaviors are influenced by the interaction of psychiatric disturbance with environmental and learning variables. The influence of environmental and learning factors over and above psychiatric illness was nicely demonstrated in a study by Matson and Mayville (2001). In this study, 135 individuals with mental retardation were assessed to determine which of several environmental and learning factors were controlling their aggressive behaviors. Environmental and learning variables were identified as controlling aggressive behaviors in 75% of the cases and, here is the important point, there was no significant difference in the extent of environmental control for individuals with mental retardation alone versus those with a dual diagnosis (i.e. mental retardation plus psychopathology). Matson and Mayville concluded that environmental and learning factors need to be considered as functional (i.e. causal) in the control of challenging behavior even when the person has a dual diagnosis.

Two cases reported by Lowry and Sovner (1992) also highlighted differing behavioral patterns in individuals with the same diagnoses, which would seem to suggest a more indirect relation between psychopathology and challenging behavior. A man and a woman, both of whom had profound mental retardation, challenging behavior (aggression, self-injury), and bi-polar (manic-depressive) disorder were observed. Now if it were the case that bi-polar disorder caused challenging behavior, then one would expect a similar behavioral pattern in both of these clients, but the reality was vastly different. One individual showed challenging behavior when depressed; the other, when manic. How could this be unless the psychiatric condition interacted with other variables to influence the pattern of challenging behavior in relation to the two phases of the disorder?

One possibility is that psychiatric conditions interact with environmental and learning variables in ways that vary across persons depending on their experiences and motivations. When depressed, for example, a person might want to be left alone, perhaps to sleep all day. If caregiver attempts to rouse the person from slumber are met with aggressive outbursts, and if these outbursts are effective in driving others away, then we can see how aggression might be shaped up as a response to being bothered. Alternatively another client might become aggressive during the manic phase when others try to interrupt or otherwise control the manic over-activity. If a well-placed punch or a prolonged rage even occasionally enables the client to break free from such attempts at control, then we would of course expect to see high rates of problem behavior associated with the manic phase of the bi-polar cycle. Following this line of reasoning, psychiatric disorders could be conceptualized as a setting event for challenging behavior. The term setting event is used here in the sense that when the person is in a certain mood or state, ordinarily benign environmental events, such as a reasonable request to get out of bed or to stop running around the house might now function as triggers or antecedents for challenging behaviors (Carr and Smith, 1995).

Consider now some of the other implicated health and medical problems. Could a toothache, ear or sinus infection, sleep disorder, or even a sore toe, increase the frequency and severity of challenging behavior? The answer is clearly yes for we can point to specific cases where such links have been demonstrated (Gunsett et al., 1989; O'Reilly and Lancioni, 2000). But is this link direct or indirect? Here the answer is not so clear.

A child with an earache may find that tugging on the ear or even a bit of head banging will bring some temporary relief. Indeed, the connection between ear infection and head banging has been recognized for a very long time (De Lissovoy, 1963). Here then is a prime example where it does seem meaningful and correct to infer that the infection was in fact the precipitating cause of the problem behavior. Such direct links might occur in other scenarios too, such as scratching to alleviate an itch, grinding an aching tooth, or picking at a wound.

In all of these scenarios, the prediction would be that once the infection, itch or pain was gone, then the problem behavior would cease. This no doubt happens in many cases, but it is also possible that what precipitates the behavior may not necessarily be all that is relevant. Challenging behaviors, regardless of why and how they might start, are nearly always likely to evoke a response from caregivers and these responses may continue to exert an influence on the problem behavior long after the precipitating event has passed. Carr and McDowell (1980) provided a classic example. They described a 10-year-old boy who began scratching in response to dermatitis. Once started, however, the behavior was shown to be maintained by social reinforcement (attention) from caregivers. This example highlights the possibility that variables related to the emergence of challenging behaviors may be quite different from those that keep the behavior going.

In other situations, the health or medical problem may act more like a setting event. When sleep deprived, for example, the person may be more likely to react to even reasonable requests from caregivers with an outburst of challenging behavior (Didden and Sigafoos, 2001). Carr and Smith (1995) described how a number of health and medical issues (menses, otitis media, fatigue, allergies, and constipation) could act as setting events for self-injury. The basic mechanism is elegant in its simplicity and easy to demonstrate. All we have to do is find a person who ordinarily has no problem waiting in line or completing a task when asked, and then look to see what happens in the same situation when the person is tired, hungry, constipated or in pain. If these conditions increase the probability of challenging behaviors in the ordinarily benign situation, then it is meaningful to conceptualize the prevailing health condition as a setting event for challenging behavior. If being tired, hungry, constipated or in pain can function as setting events for self-injury, it is almost certain that similar conditions could act as setting events for challenging behavior in general. The approach to treatment in such cases first and foremost involves providing effective medical care to redress the health problem (see Chapter 5).

Placement

The final risk factor considered in this chapter is placement. By placement we mean where the person lives, attends school, or works. In terms of living environment, the prevalence studies are consistent in showing that challenging behaviors are more prevalent in institutional as compared to community living arrangements. In Sigafoos et al. (1994), 35% of those in institutional settings were identified as having aggressive behaviors, whereas the percentage for those living in community-based group homes was only 17%. Oliver et al. (1987) reported similar trends for self-injury and the same general relation is found when comparing school and work settings. Generally, the more restrictive the setting (e.g. special school versus integrated classroom; sheltered workshop versus open or competitive employment; institution versus community-home) the higher the prevalence of challenging behavior (Griffin et al., 1987; Holloway and Sigafoos, 1999; Schroeder et al., 1997).

A first uncritical glance at these trends suggests that placement in a restrictive setting must indeed increase the risk of developing challenging behaviors. There must be something about such settings, one would think, that causes challenging behavior to emerge in more people than would otherwise be the case and any number of plausible explanations could be put forth for what the cause or causes might be. Perhaps the increased risk stems from lack of activity, or lack of choices (Kearney, Durand and Mindell, 1995). Perhaps the increased risk is related to a more general environmental impoverishment that is all too often characteristic of segregated settings, especially large institutional settings (Young et al., 2001). Alternatively the risk could stem from the presence of others with challenging behavior serving as negative role models. Perhaps instead, or in addition, challenging behavior could represent fallout from the abuse and neglect that is far too common in institutional and other restrictive settings (Sobsey, 1994).

All of these explanations are plausible, but one should be aware of the fact that the direction of the risk relation might just be wrong. That is, challenging behavior, rather than resulting from a restrictive environment, might in fact cause the person to be referred to and placed in a more restrictive setting. Over time then these more restrictive facilities would tend to accumulate a population who are there precisely because they were difficult to manage in less restrictive settings. This would account for the higher prevalence of challenging behavior in those settings.

This counter-argument has empirical support. It has long been known that challenging behavior is one of the major reasons why people end up in mental retardation institutions (Hill and Bruininks, 1984; Jacobson, 1982). Indeed, the presence of challenging behavior is a major reason why parents seek out-of-home placement for their child (Chan and Sigafoos, 2000). Similarly, it is not inconceivable that special schools tend to receive children who failed in the regular classroom and that these children often fail because of their challenging behavior. Sheltered workshops, in turn, might over time tend to employ many more people who did not make it in less restrictive job settings because of problematic behaviors. It is also the case that more restrictive settings tend to contain individuals with severe disabilities, and as we have seen, individuals with severe disabilities tend to be at greater risk for challenging behavior. The higher prevalence of challenging behavior in more restrictive settings must therefore reflect, at least to some extent, the prevailing placement practices and population demographics of those settings. This does not however mean that certain variables associated with more restrictive settings, such as a relative lack of activity and choice making, do not influence the emergence and maintenance of challenging behavior, as we shall see in Chapter 4.

Summary and conclusion

Whatever the connection between these various risk factors and challenging behavior, it is clear that challenging behavior is not a problem confined to the most severely disabled, the least skilled in terms of adaptive behavior, the old or the young, the worst institutions or the most segregated of schools or workshops. It is instead a problem that, while more commonly found in individuals who share certain of these characteristics, appears to adhere strictly to no cultural, racial, socio-economic, geographic or placement boundaries. We have seen challenging behavior in institutions, segregated schools and sheltered workshops to be sure, but also in children from good homes with loving parents, in the most inclusive of schools, and in the most open of vocational programs. What do these observations have to tell us about the importance of risk factors? For one they suggest that risk factors are part of the story, but not the whole story.

Our review of risk factors leads us to the following two conclusions: First, persons with severe mental retardation, limited or no speech, and autism or autistic-like behaviors have an increased risk for challenging behavior. Second, it would appear that risk factors could affect challenging behaviors directly, as in the case of certain acute infections, pain, and perhaps even certain syndromes, whereas in other cases the nature of the influence is more indirect.

Still, prudence would suggest that it would be wise not to draw any firm conclusions on whether the major risk factors under review in this chapter are in any way directly or even indirectly responsible for the emergence and maintenance of challenging behavior. While we have sought to outline possible indirect mechanisms, such as impairment of learning or other environmental influences, which could conceivably connect the risk factor to the challenging behavior, we acknowledge that there is much to be learned about how these factors influence challenging behavior. This is especially true of biological and medical factors and yet it is these factors that seem to hold a particularly strong explanatory appeal in many circles. From our experience, parents, teachers and care staff have often attributed a person's challenging behavior to their syndrome, to their seizure disorder, or to some other medical or psychiatric problem in a rather direct way. We are not suggesting that such explanations should be discounted, rather we argue that such factors need to be investigated before attributing them as the cause of the person's behavior problems. The current knowledge base is limited.

The influence of the variables considered to be risk factors and how they might influence the emergence and maintenance of challenging behavior is certainly worth investigating more fully. We do not completely understand the causes of challenging behavior. In our state of ignorance an open, yet skeptical, mind appears to be good policy. Yet at the same time, there seems to be enough evidence to enable us to begin to form a coherent picture of the more basic mechanisms by which these factors might influence the emergence and maintenance of challenging behavior. Developing this picture is the aim of the next chapter.

A theory of challenging behavior

Introduction

In any attempt to develop a systematic explanation or theory of some aspect of human conduct there is a need to ensure that the behaviors to be explained can in fact be identified in ways that are reliable and valid. We have already noted the difficulties of identifying challenging behaviors in ways that are reliable and valid, but if we have done our job sufficiently well, you should at least now have a better understanding of the behaviors that are considered challenging and how these have been defined, identified, classified and described. In review, we are concerned with the major types and forms of severe behavior problems (aggression, self-injury, extreme tantrums, property destruction and other disruptive acts) that are highly prevalent and consistently identified as challenging in populations of people with developmental disabilities. We are further focused on presenting a theory to explain why some individuals have persistent, frequent and severe patterns of challenging behaviors, while others have little or no such behavior in their repertoire. We are not concerned, in this chapter at least, with explaining why any particular instance of challenging behavior has occurred, although the theory or perspective that is offered in this chapter may in fact provide the clinician with a fruitful way of analyzing specific instances of challenging behavior.

From Chapter 2, you should have a sense of the many and varied factors that are associated with an increased risk of challenging behavior. You should also have a sense of some of the possible mechanisms that might explain why and how these factors influence the development and persistence of challenging behavior. The task for this chapter is to integrate these possible mechanisms into a coherent theory of challenging behavior to explain the high prevalence of such behaviors in persons with developmental disabilities. The theory or perspective[1] outlined in this chapter should also help to explain individual differences in the topography, frequency and severity of challenging behavior among individuals with developmental disabilities.

Explaining challenging behavior

Theories to explain challenging behavior are plentiful. Those responsible for supporting individuals with developmental disabilities and challenging behaviors must be able to distinguish the good theory from the bad, the complete from the incomplete, the sense from the nonsense. A good and complete explanation or theory is marked by its ability to account for the many and varied facts about challenging behaviors that were reviewed in Chapters 1 and 2 as well as its ability to generate new and more effective approaches to assessment and intervention.

Bad theories, and the ineffective treatments that they spawn, are one likely reason why challenging behaviors remain a major problem in developmental disability services. Prior to the mid-1960s, for example, it was fashionable to account for challenging behavior in terms of anxiety, guilt and self-punishment. The theory was that challenging behaviors stemmed from some deep-seated emotional problem or inner turmoil. Such theorizing was consistent with a prevailing belief that autism and related developmental disabilities were essentially psychological, rather than neurological (Bettelheim, 1949, 1955, 1974). In this tradition, problem behaviors are said to arise in part from the failure to resolve the inner conflicts that besiege the individual. Treatments based on this theory involved unconditional valuing presumably to absolve the individual of their guilt. Operationally, this approach to treatment often took the form of providing attention and comfort to the individual in response to challenging behavior. It is now clear that the theory was wrong and the treatments it fostered ineffective. In fact Lovaas and his colleagues (Lovaas et al., 1965; Lovaas and Simmons, 1969) showed that treatments based on such theories actually made challenging behavior worse.

In considering various theories and treatments for challenging behavior it is wise to remain skeptical until the evidence can be evaluated. This is because the field as a whole is littered with a long history of unsubstantiated claims, promises of miracle cures and crackpot therapies. Facilitated communication (Weiss, 2002) and Gentle Teaching (McGee, 1992) are just two recent examples of treatments that continue to be advocated despite considerable evidence that both are not only ineffective, but also potentially harmful (Bailey, 1992; Jacobson, Mulick and Schwartz, 1995; Mudford, 1995). One reason why the field is vulnerable to fads is because new yet unproven treatments are often justified by reference to an elaborate and appealing, but incorrect, theory of human nature.

Of course not all theories about challenging behavior are necessarily bad in the sense of being incorrect. Some are simply incomplete. When challenging behavior is attributed to the developmental disability – as in the common refrain that the boy bangs his head because he has autism – the explanation is incomplete because challenging behaviors are not restricted to individuals with developmental disabilities (De Lissovoy, 1963; Winchel and Stanley, 1991). In addition, not all individuals with developmental disabilities engage in challenging behavior. Although insufficient, there must be something about having a developmental disability that increases the risk of challenging behavior as discussed in Chapter 2. A better or more general theory is therefore needed to explain how and why the presence of a developmental disability can increase the risk that a person will develop challenging behavior.

Similarly, the high prevalence of self-biting in Lesch-Nyhan syndrome, hand wringing in Rett syndrome, and skin picking with Prader-Willi syndrome, for example, suggests that challenging behaviors may represent unique syndrome-specific behavioral phenotypes. Although this theory may be useful in directing attention to genetic variables that no doubt influence behavior directly or indirectly, the evidence on the existence of such phenotypes is hardly conclusive (Clarke and Boer, 1998). It is also important to realize that similar forms of challenging behavior are seen in individuals who do not have the associated syndrome and that not all individuals with these syndromes show the supposedly characteristic behaviors to the same extent. Thus a theory of challenging behavior based on behavioral phenotypes alone is incomplete because it does not explain how genetic factors interact with other variables to account for the many individual differences in the topography, frequency, and severity of challenging behavior both within and across specific developmental disability syndromes.

As with phenotypes, the theory that challenging behaviors are manifestations of psychiatric disorders or caused by health and medical problems could be useful in directing attention to important physiological and biological factors affecting the individual. However, merely attributing the challenging behavior to a psychiatric disorder or to an illness is incomplete because similar behaviors are seen in people without such disorders or illnesses and not everyone with a particular diagnosis necessarily manifests behaviors that would be appropriately classified as challenging.

Thus theories related to genetic, psychiatric, and health/medical causes are useful, but incomplete. They are useful in that they direct attention to potentially important variables, but incomplete because they do not explain how these variables interact with other factors (such as individual learning histories) to account for the development, persistence and relatively high prevalence of challenging behavior among individuals with developmental disabilities overall. Other more specific theories, such as the hypotheses that challenging behaviors are caused by impoverished environments, represent a form of communication or arise from social skills deficits, can also be seen as incomplete for similar reasons. What is needed then is a more general theory or perspective that will enable the evidence supportive of these specific theories to be integrated. To this end it is important to further clarify the nature of challenging behavior.

The nature of challenging behavior

In conceptualizing the nature of challenging behavior in individuals with developmental disabilities, it is important to consider whether such behaviors are in fact determined largely by the nature of the person's disability. It is also important to consider whether or not challenging behaviors are of a fundamentally different kind than other forms of behaviors.

If the behaviors of individuals with developmental disabilities are determined largely by the nature of their disability then we would expect their behaviors, and the reasons for these behaviors, to be vastly different from those of people without developmental disabilities. If, on the other hand, the behaviors and the reasons for these behaviors have more to do with general principles that influence the behavior of all people regardless of whether or not they have a disability, then whatever qualitative differences there might be between the behavior of people with and without developmental disabilities may be relatively less important than first imagined, at least in terms of trying to explain behavior.

Much research has focused on differences between people with and without disabilities; relatively less has explored the similarities (Matson and Mulick, 1991). As a result, the differences tend to be highlighted, whereas the similarities may often go unnoticed. Differences are the figures that stand out against a background of similarities. The lure of differences is often irresistible in attempting to explain challenging behavior in persons with developmental disabilities. The theory or perspective being developed in this chapter is focused more on similarities because people with disabilities are first and foremost human beings and their behavior, including their challenging behavior, must therefore be responsive to the same basic principles that affect all human behavior. To believe otherwise is to assign individuals with developmental disabilities to some "other" category. A focus on similarities does not, however, prevent us from considering how these basic principles interact with individual characteristics, including characteristics related to the person's disability, to influence challenging behavior.

Behavior is anything a person says or does. In this respect then challenging behavior is similar to other forms of behavior, be it walking, talking, dressing or eating. It is in the attempt to account for challenging behavior that different types of explanations seem to be necessary. From an early age, children are asked to account for their actions. Adults often teach this incidentally when they ask questions such as *Why did you do that?* and *Why did you say that?* The fact that such questions are routinely asked, and children are expected to answer, illustrates the widely held belief that there is in fact a reason for the things that a person says and does. This does not mean that the reasons given by those so questioned are necessarily accurate or correct because the person may not necessarily know the true reasons for the things they do. Indeed, a careful analysis of the variables that control behavior – that is, the real reasons for the behavior – show that these lie in the environment, even though they may be attributed to some internal agent (Skinner, 1945). A child might say that she did such and such because she wanted to or felt like it, but a more thorough analysis would seek to identify those variables in the environment that explain why the child wanted to or felt like doing that particular behavior.

Although people generally seem to expect that there will be perfectly good reasons for most behaviors, there also seem to be cases when the form of the behavior is so bizarre that it is placed beyond the realm of normal human functioning. The challenging behaviors of people with developmental disabilities are often placed in this category. This is understandable because challenging behaviors often appear so strange that they must surely be unlike any other "normal" behavior. To the casual observer it is difficult if not impossible to conceive of any logical explanation for why someone would slap or bite himself or lash out at caregivers, for example. Such behavior, it is often heard, must surely represent some bizarre manifestation of the person's disability.

However, simply because a behavior looks bizarre or seems irrational does not make it inexplicable nor of some fundamentally different kind. Challenging behavior is first and foremost human behavior and it is affected by the same variables that influence all human behavior. These variables operate in accordance with basic known principles (Herrnstein, 1970; Skinner, 1953). The basic principles hold whether the individual is aware of them or not and whether the behavior is considered to be adaptive or maladaptive, rational or irrational, typical or bizarre. While behaviors are often classified in such terms for clinical purposes, experimental data show there to be two general types of behavior: Respondent behavior and operant behavior. This typology does not respect the distinctions implied by the adaptive–maladaptive dichotomy.

Respondent behavior and operant behavior

Respondent behaviors are elicited by a prior specific stimulus and usually involve the autonomic nervous system. Common examples of respondent behaviors include the knee-jerk and eye-blink reflexes that occur in response to a tap on the knee and puff of air to the eyelid, respectively. Respondent behaviors also include physiological reactions such as salivation, perspiration, and heart rate. These too can be elicited by presentation of a specific stimulus such as food in the mouth for salivation or a painful stimulus for perspiration and heart rate. Emotional responses, such as fear, anxiety – and yes even joy and satisfaction – are also often appropriately viewed as examples of respondent behavior when it can be shown that these responses occur due to the presentation of some prior specific stimulus. The ability of certain prior stimuli to elicit an associated respondent behavior is a given provided that the person's nervous system is functioning as it should, which is not always the case for individuals with developmental disabilities.

New eliciting associations between stimuli and responses can be established through a process known as classical or Pavlovian conditioning. Put some food in a hungry child's mouth and she will begin to salivate. This is automatic and requires no experience or learning history. At the same time, however, other new associations can begin to form. If the food tastes particularly good to the child at the time – either because they are particularly hungry or because the food just happens to be especially preferred – then the feeding routine and all the paraphernalia that goes along with it will come to be associated with good tastes, good feelings and positive emotional behaviors. The child will not only start to salivate prior to receiving the food, but will also get excited (e.g. smile, giggle, flap hands, and bounce up and down) as the tell-tale signs of a coming meal appear (e.g. the smell of the food, the sight of the parent dishing up the meal, a spoon full of food moving towards the child's mouth). Should the food taste bad, however, then the situation will come to be associated with bad tastes, bad feelings and negative emotional reactions. If the parent persists and forces the child to consume what to the child is a dreadful substance, then over time the entire feeding routine can come to elicit reactions that might be properly termed fear or anxiety and this in turn can help set the occasion for other (operant) behaviors that enable the individual to escape from or avoid the now aversive situation.

Operant behaviors are controlled by their consequences and are said to involve voluntary responses. Operant behavior is generally what we think of when we use terms such as conduct, action, responses or behavior. Walking, talking, dressing, preparing a meal, mailing a letter, driving to the park, swimming, typing a letter; these are all examples of operant behaviors whose frequency is determined by the nature of the consequences that have followed such acts in the past. We write letters to people who respond in kind and stop writing to people who never reply. These are operant behaviors in the sense that they operate on the environment to produce certain outcomes or consequences (Skinner, 1953).

Operant behaviors are learned. There is no specific prior stimulus that elicits the response as in the case of respondent behavior. In the operant paradigm, new responses are established through the process of operant conditioning, which involves setting the opportunity or occasion for the response and arranging for certain types of reinforcing consequences when the response occurs. Through operant conditioning, responses can also be brought under stimulus control in the sense that the response will be more or less likely to occur in the presence of a particular stimulus. A child might very quickly learn to ask for a treat from his grandfather rather than from his mother if these two adults are associated with very different outcomes, such as if grandfather always gives treats, but mother rarely does so.

Operant and respondent behaviors can interact in complex ways. Consider the mealtime scenario outlined previously. When a reinforcing consequence is provided it will elicit physiological responses, such as salivation, and establish new stimulus–response associations through the process of classical conditioning. Whatever behavior the hungry child happened to be doing at the time that a preferred edible is received will also come to be strengthened through the process of operant conditioning. Now consider what could happen when the mealtime is associated with bad tasting and non-preferred foods. Respondent behaviors that we might call fear and anxiety could be conditioned to this situation. The child might look visibly upset and cry at the sight of a spoon loaded with spinach, for example. If the consequences of such emotional reactions are that the parent withdraws the disliked food, then crying could become established as an operant behavior related to the withdrawal of the foul tasting substance. The interaction of respondent and operant conditioning might then explain how behaviors in general and challenging behaviors in particular develop and persist.

Once a behavior has occurred, regardless of why it has occurred, it will have consequences and certain types of consequences have powerful and predictable effects on the behavior. The tendency to repeat a behavior or to engage in a particular behavior, rather than act in some alternative way, depends on the probability that certain types of consequences have followed that behavior in the past. Two types of consequences influence the frequency and strength of behavior. These are reinforcing consequences and punishing consequences.

Reinforcement and punishment

All responses produce consequences. Some of these consequences have no effect on behavior and can be considered neutral. Other consequences function to increase or strengthen responses. These consequences are known as reinforcers. Punishers, in contrast, function to decrease or weaken behavior. Human behavior is primarily shaped by its relation to reinforcing and punishing consequences. Such consequences can alter the future probability or frequency as well as the topography or form of behavior.

Reinforcement and punishment refer to a relation between a class of consequences and a class of responses. A particular consequence is a reinforcer only if it increases the probability or frequency of responses that have led to that consequence in the past. Similarly, a consequence is a punisher only if it decreases the future probability or frequency of responses that have led to that consequence in the past. An everyday example of reinforcement is the common tendency to return to restaurants where one has previously eaten good food. An everyday example of punishment is the tendency to avoid restaurants that serve bad meals. Whether or not a consequence is a reinforcer or a punisher depends solely upon whether or not it increases or decreases the future probability or frequency of the response upon which it is contingent. Reinforcers and punishers cannot be identified independently of their effects on behavior.

There are two types of reinforcing and punishing consequences; primary and secondary. Primary reinforcers include consequences that satisfy biological drives, such as hunger, thirst, and sex. Primary punishers include aversive stimuli that cause pain or discomfort. The reinforcing and punishing effects of such consequences are not dependent upon a history of association through respondent or operant conditioning. A hungry person does not have to learn the value of food, nor does the thirsty person need to learn the value of water. And so any behaviors that have led to these consequences in the past will tend to increase in frequency whenever the person is hungry or thirsty. Similarly, a person does not have to learn the punishing effects of a painful stimulus or conversely the reinforcing effects of escaping from or avoiding a painful stimulus. As a result, any behaviors that have led to escape from or avoidance of pain will tend to increase in frequency whenever a primary punishing stimulus is present.

In contrast, secondary or conditioned reinforcers and secondary or conditioned punishers acquire their repertoire altering effects as a result of learning. A person probably learns the value of attention or money because these are associated with so many different primary reinforcers. Gaining the attention of a caregiver comes to be conditioned as a secondary reinforcer in part because it is a necessary part of gaining access to the wide range of primary reinforcers that are mediated by others (e.g. food, comfort, pain relief, etc.). Over time attention comes to be valued in its own right and we then say that the child is appropriately socialized or has "bonded" with the caregiver.

Secondary punishers, such as a verbal reprimand, acquire the ability to alter behavior by prior association with a primary punisher. A child who is spanked and scolded for touching precious objects in the house, for example, will be less likely to touch such objects in the future, provided that the spanking itself was sufficiently aversive. Given sufficient pairings of the primary punisher with a scolding, the verbal reprimand itself should acquire the ability to suppress behavior. There are other likely effects beyond mere response suppression that will likely arise from such conditioning, however. Specifically, the child might also come to feel anxious in situations that have been associated with verbal reprimands and seek to escape from and avoid such situations. Avoidance may take the form of inhibiting the tendency to touch precious objects. Inhibiting a response that is otherwise strong is a form of self-control. People with developmental disabilities may have greater difficulty learning such inhibitions.

Exactly what behaviors an individual will emit to escape from and avoid aversive situations will depend on a variety of factors, such as how aversive the situation is to the individual, the behaviors that are available in the person's repertoire, and the consequences that have followed each of these available response options in the past. This variety of factors will be discussed in more detail in later sections of this chapter. The important point to bear in mind at this point is that people differ in their susceptibility to various consequences and in their susceptibility to operant and respondent conditioning. What functions as a reinforcing consequence for one person may be either neutral or punishing for another. The ease and speed with which behavior can be shaped varies tremendously from person to person as does the ease and speed with which secondary reinforcers and punishers can be established.

In general, it seems more difficult to establish secondary reinforcers and punishers in individuals with developmental disabilities and this, in turn, makes it more difficult to shape the behavior of individuals with developmental disabilities. Individual differences in susceptibility to conditioning are no doubt related to the presence of physical, sensory and cognitive impairments as noted in Chapter 2. The difficulties in establishing conditioned reinforcers and punishers often make it seem as if people with developmental disabilities do not have the same drives or motivations as other people; the reasons for their actions can thus seem bizarre and inexplicable.

Behaviors that are controlled or influenced by certain types of consequent stimuli often appear to be more natural and understandable than behaviors controlled by other more obscure or idiosyncratic forms of reinforcement and punishment. It seems easier to understand the behavior of a child who is content to play for hours with toys because we appreciate the value of toys to children. In contrast, it is often more difficult to imagine the motivation of a child who is content to sit and rock back and forth for hours and hours. Yet the behavior of both children may be understandable when the reinforcing consequences responsible for their actions are identified. Behavior is explained when the reinforcing or punishing stimuli that influence the behavior are identified. If challenging behavior is maintained by its consequences (see Chapter 6), then the only thing that could set it apart from other behavior is its topography.

In summary, studies on operant conditioning have demonstrated that consequences can have powerful and predictable effects on behavior (see the *Journal of the Experimental Analysis of Behavior*, 1958 to present and the *Journal of Applied Behavior Analysis*, 1968 to present). In fact, the probability or frequency of a behavior is determined largely by the consistency, timing and schedule with which reinforcing and punishing consequences have followed that behavior in the past (Ferster and Skinner, 1957; Herrnstein, 1970). Our theory rests on the assumption that challenging behavior is not fundamentally different from other forms of human behavior and it is therefore shaped by primary and secondary reinforcers. This view is consistent with Ted Carr's (Carr, 1977; Carr et al., 1994) argument that challenging behaviors have a function or purpose. In this context, function or purpose refers to the reinforcing consequences that maintain the behavior.

This theory also implies that frequent episodes of challenging behavior emerge and are maintained when there is a favorable ratio of reinforcement over punishment. One issue that needs to be considered in more detail then is why the prevailing contingencies of reinforcement have shaped topographies that are challenging as opposed to other more acceptable forms of conduct. Understanding the factors that determine the extent of a person's behavioral repertoire – and the probability of expression for individual responses within that repertoire – will help to explain how it is that topographies of behaviors considered challenging come to be selected instead of or in addition to other less problematic forms.

Behavioral repertoire

Behavior, as noted before, is anything a person says or does. A behavioral repertoire can therefore be thought of as all the responses or behaviors available to the individual. In the field of developmental disabilities, estimates of the person's repertoire are typically sought through an assessment of adaptive behavior functioning using one or more standardized rating scales (see Browder, 2001 for a review).

In Chapter 1 you learned that developmental disability is characterized by substantial deficits in adaptive behavior functioning. The term substantial means that these deficits are big, important, and meaningful. When deficits in adaptive behavior functioning are substantial it also means that the behavioral repertoire is relatively small and restricted. Put more simply and compared with people without disabilities, individuals with developmental disabilities have fewer and more restricted forms of behaviors in their repertoire.

Many factors probably contribute to the relatively restricted behavioral repertoires characteristic of individuals with developmental disabilities. One of these is no doubt the degree of intellectual impairment. Intellectual ability and the extent of one's behavioral repertoire are probably related. B.F. Skinner (1968) defined intelligence as the ability to acquire and maintain a large repertoire of behavior without confusion. Persons with more severe intellectual impairments would therefore be expected to acquire responses more slowly, maintain fewer responses, and experience confusion in terms of integrating or chaining separate responses into complex skills. The ease and speed with which new behaviors are acquired and integrated presumably depends, at least to some extent, on learning ability, which is in turn related to the degree of intellectual disability. As discussed in Chapter 2, intellectual disability is associated with an impaired ability to learn and the impairment in learning hinders the ease and speed with which new responses are acquired. Intellectual impairment is also associated with attentional and memory problems that make it more difficult to maintain behaviors in the repertoire without confusion. In short, individuals with developmental disabilities have smaller and more restricted behavioral repertories because of the learning difficulties associated with the condition.

Physical and sensory capabilities also no doubt influence the extent of the behavioral repertoire. A person with severe cerebral palsy may be physically incapable of acquiring skills that require certain topographies or forms of gross and fine motor actions. A blind person might be incapable of learning responses that depend on sight and a deaf person will obviously have more difficulty learning responses that depend on hearing. The presence and degree of physical and sensory impairments could therefore directly affect the number and forms of behaviors in the repertoire.

Genetic syndromes and psychiatric disability also affect the repertoire rather directly by making some responses more likely than others, but some syndrome or psychiatric disorders may influence the repertoire

more indirectly by altering the reinforcing effects of certain consequences, reducing inhibitions, and altering the perception of sensory
stimuli. All of these potential influences might disrupt acquisition, maintenance and the ordering of responses in the repertoire.

In addition to the degree of intellectual, physical, sensory and/or psychiatric impairment, the opportunities and experiences afforded the individual
with developmental disability will no doubt have an effect on their behavioral repertoire. In some settings, individuals with developmental
disabilities may have insufficient or ineffective opportunities for learning
and their lifestyles overall may be characterized by a restricted range of
experiences. Institutions, sheltered workshops and other segregated settings are notorious for stifling individual potential by restricting
opportunities (Holloway and Sigafoos, 1999; Young et al., 1998). There is
little doubt that some such facilities present an impoverished environment
that must severely limit people's behavioral repertoires (Blatt and Kaplan,
1974; Thompson, 1977). But more typical and inclusive settings by themselves do not necessarily create the right conditions for skill development.
Even living in the most enriched of environments with the support of well-
meaning and loving parents, teachers and therapists can limit a person's
development if these carers do things for the individual rather than provide
opportunities for learning. This is a form of benevolent enslavement that
just as surely restricts the person's skill development. The physical and
social conditions of life might therefore constrict or enhance skill development, which is why quality of life issues are important to the understanding
and treatment of challenging behavior as we shall see in Chapter 4.

It can be helpful to view the behavioral repertoire in terms of action,
conduct function, or purpose (Carr et al., 1994; Lee, 1988). Put in collo-
quial terms, we use our behaviors to achieve certain (reinforcing) ends.
People with the motor skills to walk will walk of course, but when they do
so they are often walking somewhere to do something. They might walk
to the post office to mail a letter, to the grocery store for some milk, to a
café for lunch, or to the park to feed the ducks. Walking, in this example,
is part of the act of mailing a letter, shopping for groceries, having lunch,
and feeding the ducks. People with other skills and longer distances to
travel might drive a car, hail a cab or take the bus.

Each of these ambulation options, be it walking, driving, or even roller
skating can have the same function or purpose. Specific forms of challenging behavior, such as head banging, throwing objects, or hitting
others, might also be viewed as having a function or purpose. A child
might cry, hit, or throw objects in an attempt to coerce his parents into
letting him stay up at night to watch television. Function or purpose, as
we have noted previously in this chapter, refers to the reinforcing consequences that maintain the action.

Typically, as the above examples illustrate, different forms or topographies are used to accomplish the same function and the same forms might be used for different purposes. Depending on the weather a person might walk or drive to the post office. At other times these same response options (walking or driving) might be enlisted to get the person to the grocery store or café or park. What is typical overall, however, is not necessarily characteristic of individuals with developmental disabilities. As we have emphasized throughout this chapter, people with developmental disabilities are likely to have fewer different forms or topographies in their repertoires. This means they have fewer response options to call upon for any given function or purpose.

Challenging behavior as a response option

We can now turn to the issue of how it is that challenging behaviors enter and even dominate the repertoires of so many individuals with developmental disabilities. It may at first seem odd that there would be a high prevalence of challenging behaviors among a group of people who have comparatively fewer behaviors in their overall repertoires. With fewer forms overall would not one expect there to be fewer challenging behaviors also? To understand this apparent contradiction, it is important to review the common forms of challenging behaviors that were catalogued in Chapter 1.

Looking back at Tables 1.1, 1.2 and 1.3, one might notice that many of the most common forms of challenging behaviors involve relatively imprecise gross motor acts such as hitting, biting and scratching, rather than some more complex sequence of behavior. It is possible that these forms are shaped from the rather undifferentiated movements that emerge during early development. If so, the raw material from which challenging forms emerge is present in the repertories of most individuals from an early age. It is also important to recall from Chapter 1 that episodes of challenging behavior generally involve the repetition of forms and escalation in the intensity of these forms, rather than more complex chains of multiple and coordinated response forms.

Challenging behaviors might not so much enter the repertoire as emerge from the store of physiological, reflexive, stereotyped movements and emotional reactions that develop in infancy. Crying – initially a physiological response – may develop into persistent screaming if parents come to respond more consistently to intense rather than weak cries. Through a similar shaping process certain gross motor responses, such as flailing the arms and legs about when excited or angry, may be transformed into the more directed (and intense) forms of hitting and kicking.

Admittedly this analysis is speculative, but if it has any merit, then one would expect challenging behaviors to emerge among young children in general and not just among young children with developmental disabilities. And this appears to be precisely what happens. Young children with and without developmental disabilities cry and sometimes the cry is shaped up to become so persistent and intense that it may be viewed as challenging. Young children with and without disabilities kick their legs when excited or angry. Sometimes the excitement or anger, and the associated hitting and kicking, may become so intense that it is considered aggressive. What distinguishes one group of children from the other is that challenging behaviors tend to persist in many more children with developmental disabilities as compared to those without. Why is this?

Our view is that challenging behaviors persist more in children with developmental disabilities as compared to their peers without disabilities for two related reasons. First, challenging behaviors are easily shaped from the physiological, reflexive, stereotyped and emotional responses that develop in infancy. Second, and unlike their typically developing peers, children with developmental disabilities have so much more difficulty learning alternative behaviors. People with developmental disabilities have more difficulty learning and we have more difficulty teaching them the communication, self-care, play and social skills that others seem to acquire without explicit or deliberate instruction. Although children without disabilities may certainly develop challenging behaviors in their early years and these behaviors may indeed persist, in many cases any such challenging behaviors are displaced or replaced as the child's behavioral repertoire expands. Crying becomes less common as the child develops language, for example.

An inverse relation exists between the size and extent of the behavioral repertoire and the frequency and severity of challenging behavior, as noted in Chapter 2. Consider for example, the findings of a study published by one of the authors in the journal *Education and Training in Mental Retardation and Developmental Disabilities* (Sigafoos, 2000). The study tracked 13 preschoolers with developmental disabilities over three years beginning when the children were about four years of age. Every six months the children's adaptive and maladaptive behaviors were assessed. At each round of data collection, higher ratings of adaptive behaviors, especially in the communication domain, were associated with less severe challenging behavior and vice verse. Similar results have been found time and time again as we documented in Chapter 2. The high prevalence of challenging behavior among individuals with developmental disabilities could therefore reflect the fact that challenging behaviors are relatively easily shaped from existing reflexive, physiological, and emotional responses, whereas alternative adaptive skills are so much more complex and hence so much more difficult for children with developmental disabilities to learn.

Summary and conclusion

We are now in a position to provide a summative statement of the theory. It is a theory about the nature of challenging behavior. The theory states that the relatively higher frequency and prevalence of challenging behavior among individuals with developmental disabilities can be understood in terms of the response options available to the person. When the behavioral repertoire is restricted, there are fewer response options, but there is still the need to respond. Responses will still be called forth so to speak. There will still be stimuli impinging upon the person that elicit respondent behavior and stimuli that set the occasion for operant behavior. Behavior will occur in response to these stimuli, but the form that the response takes will of course be constrained by the forms available in the repertoire. A person can only do what they can do and when forced to act people generally choose the preferred response option. Preference and choice in this context simply mean that the response is determined. When a response occurs it has consequences. If the consequence happens to be reinforcing, then that response will be more likely to occur in the future under similar conditions. In many cases, when the conditions next arise, the individual may have no choice but to choose challenging behavior because their repertoire does not include any alternative forms that could serve the same function or purpose as challenging behavior, or these alternatives are not as effective as challenging behavior.

Challenging behavior is therefore likely to emerge as a frequent response option when any one of several conditions exist: (1) When appropriate alternative forms are absent or deficient; (2) when alternative forms are more difficult; (3) when alternative forms fail to produce reinforcement; and (4) when reinforcement for alternative forms is less immediate or consistent than it is for challenging behavior. When any one or some combination of these conditions exists, challenging behavior is likely to occur as the more probable response option. Challenging behaviors occur when current impinging stimuli elicit a response or set the occasion for a response as a result of prior respondent or operant conditioning, respectively. We believe that challenging behavior is highly prevalent among people with developmental disabilities because the four conditions outlined above pervade the lives of people with developmental disabilities.

In summary, challenging behavior is no different from other types of behaviors. It may seem irrational and maladaptive, but that is only because observers may not have access to the various factors, many of which are related to the person's developmental and learning history, that have shaped the behavior. The theory developed in this chapter is general. It is not specific to challenging behavior, but in considering the extension of this general behavioral theory to challenging behavior the implications for assessment and treatment should start to become obvious. The remainder of this book considers these implications in more detail while always attempting to highlight the general theoretical principles that underlie assessment and intervention. We continue with this more detailed discussion in the next chapter by considering ethical and quality of life issues.

Note

1. We do not claim originality for the theory or perspective developed in this chapter. Rather, it is derived from behavioral psychology and heavily influenced by the work of experimental and applied behavior analysts, such as B.F. Skinner, R.J. Herrnstein, Travis Thompson, Ted Carr and Brian Iwata.

PART 2

FUNDAMENTAL ISSUES IN SERVICE PROVISION

CHAPTER 4
Ethical considerations and quality of life issues

Introduction

Up to this point we have focused on understanding the nature of challenging behavior: what it is, how widespread it is in the lives of people with developmental disabilities, common risk factors and specific reasons for its occurrence. As we start to consider the provision of services to reduce or prevent the problems of challenging behavior, it is appropriate to review the critical ethical and quality of life considerations that underpin best practice in this field.

At first glance, the concepts of quality of life, ethical practices and principles and the phenomenon of challenging behavior appear to be quite disparate. However, as we will see in our review of the conceptual and descriptive literature, they are integrally linked to each other. For example, there is ample evidence of the connection between low quality of life indicators (e.g. communicatively impoverished environments) and increased levels of challenging behaviors, and conversely, the achievement of more positive social repertoires when a supportive and positive environment is provided.

Horner (1980) conducted what has got to be the seminal study in this area. In this classic study, Horner focused on five school-aged individuals who had profound disability, lived in an institution, and had a history of challenging behaviors. Horner found that the provision of an enriched environment (for example, toys and objects of interest) along with the systematic use of differential reinforcement techniques produced important reductions in observed self-stimulatory, injurious and other antisocial behaviors as well as increased object-directed adaptive behaviors. This significant study provided a basis for improvements in disability services and educational programs predicated on the relationship that exists among contexts, activities and social skills and the concept that the quality of the living and learning environment is central to effective behavior support.

However, it is also possible to view the link between ethical practices, quality of life experiences and challenging behaviors from another angle. It appears that the demonstration of increased or entrenched challenging behaviors may result in reduced life opportunities as a function of experiences such as physical restraint, segregation, or limited access to the wider community, especially if humane and responsible procedures for positive support are not followed (Horner, Diemer and Brazeau, 1992; Lehr and Brown, 1996). Instead of an environmental trigger to challenging behavior, as we mentioned above, a problem situation may be exacerbated by the consequences of the behavior for the social environment, including risk to the community, possible self-harm and other negative outcomes. Unfortunately, this scenario can lead to a counterproductive and negative cycle of restriction. For example, if a person permanently lives in a locked ward, is unable to model socially acceptable interactions, and instead is exposed to inappropriate behaviors on a daily basis, it could be argued that there is little chance that they will break out of what may become a vicious cycle of maladaptive behavior. Their challenging repertoire therefore functions to hamper the range and quality of activities and interactions they participate in, interfering with their broader membership of society and potentially setting the scene for more established and frequent antisocial behaviors.

As we note later, some authors have argued that there may be occasions when it is necessary for intrusive strategies, such as brief restraint or contingent aversive stimulation, if positive approaches alone have not worked. This decision brings with it a raft of legal, moral and ethical implications. The reader interested in this area is referred to an excellent appendix in Alberto and Troutman (1999) containing statements by five relevant professional associations regarding the use of aversive interventions. Having recognized the complexity inherent in this area, in the next section we explore in detail the relationship among quality of life considerations and ethical approaches to the treatment of challenging behavior.

Quality of life

Quality of life has been aptly described as "the slipperiest species in the conceptual zoo" by Hibbins and Compton (1994), an observation confirmed by a recent scan of web and library resources on the topic. In this chapter, it is not our intention to become bogged down in debate about the nature or definition of quality of life (QOL). Rather, we are interested in the connection between QOL indicators and ethical aspects in the provision of positive behavior support (PBS). To this end, we will adopt Schalock's (2000) recent definition:

> Quality of life is a concept that reflects a person's desired conditions of living related to eight core dimensions of one's life: emotional well-being, interpersonal relationships, material well-being, personal development, physical well-being, self-determination, social inclusion and rights. (p. 121)

Two elements that complement and overlay this definition are ecological complexity and the contribution of self-advocacy.

As we note throughout this book, intervention for challenging behavior can best be provided at a number of levels within the ecology of the individual, including the various settings in which they spend their time. Risley (1996) provides a thorough analysis of the range of micro and macro factors that impact QOL, concluding that "a high quality of life could be mostly achieved by life arrangements – rather than by behavior change" (p. 428). For example, a change in living arrangement from a congregate situation to one in which individual habits and lifestyle choices are honored has the potential to significantly improve multiple layers of a person's QOL. In concert with this idea, Horner (2000) has noted the potential for expansion of behavior support, with impacts for individual problem behavior right through to systemic, governmental and cultural changes in accepted approaches to social behavior (p. 103). Indeed, Horner notes that "The signature feature of positive behavior support (PBS) has been a committed focus on fixing environments, not people" (2000, p. 97). Along the same lines, Turnbull et al. (2002) recently used a detailed case study to argue that school-wide positive behavior support has direct relevance for all students, and can involve three levels of intensity: universal (whole school: reduce or eliminate problem behaviors), group support, and individual support. This model is entirely consistent with the ecological connectedness theme we have grappled with so far in this chapter (see http://pbis.org/ for valuable links and resources in the PBS field).

In the 1997 Amendments to the Individuals with Disabilities Education Act (IDEA), for example, the American Congress specifically provided favored status to what they termed "positive behavioral interventions, strategies and supports" for students with problem repertoires (Turnbull et al., 2000). This decision was a powerful statement about the scientific efficacy of the model, despite continuing debate about issues of reliability in implementation. In their examination of the legal implications of this legislation, Drasgow and Yell (2001) highlighted the vital contribution of functional behavioral assessment processes to the development of positive behavior support plans, and the ongoing need for such assessment and intervention to be data-based as well as contextually and socially valid.

An analysis of the social validity of PBS was recently undertaken by Kincaid et al. (2002). A total of 374 team members (including parents, teachers, school administrators and direct care workers) rated the outcomes of positive behavior support processes for 78 individuals with varying disabilities they had worked with (age range 3–22 years). In this study, it was particularly interesting to see the dual focus on multiple levels of need, intervention support and reported behavioral outcomes, and the relationship of this intervention to quality of life indicators. The results strongly supported the effectiveness of PBS, with a high proportion of participants indicating that problem behaviors were less severe, occurred less frequently and for shorter durations after PBS. From a practical point of view, the respondents were also generally pleased with the various aspects related to implementation of PBS, including elements of contextual fit and the development of positive alternatives for challenging behaviors (Kincaid et al., 2002). Notwithstanding a number of differences in the responses of different participant groups, the authors noted moderate improvements in the overall index of QOL as well as each of the five domains that were assessed (interpersonal relationships, self-determination, social inclusion, personal well-being and emotional well-being), following PBS implementation.

Socially valid and sustained behavioral changes are best achieved in real-life contexts, with natural supports. The impacts of such changes for QOL, similarly, should be evaluated in terms of all the experiences and interactions that impact upon the individual. This approach to the total assessment of lifestyle is usually termed person-centered planning and will be discussed a little later in this chapter.

The level of self-advocacy and self-determination a person experiences, likewise, has the potential to impact QOL and, implicitly, one's social repertoire. It stands to reason that the more an individual believes they are being heard and have the opportunity to represent their views, make choices and have control over life events, the more likely it is that contentment and satisfaction will follow (Westling and Fox, 2000). In their analysis of issues in the achievement of true self-determination for people with severe disabilities, Brown et al. (1998) underlined the importance of supporting autonomy within a framework of societal and personal connection. For example, in relation to educational programming, "objectives should more meaningfully reflect how students can increase control of their activities and experiences, affect their environment, and with dignity partake in the interdependence that other citizens enjoy" (1998, p. 24).

Following this line of thinking, it is helpful for educators and other professionals to reflect upon the degree to which their actions and supports facilitate self-determined behavior in people with developmental disabilities, including autonomy, self-regulation, self-realization and empowerment (Wehmeyer, 1999, p. 57). Similarly, how can parents, professionals and self-advocates work together to increase the power and control of people with disabilities in our community, across the life span (Wehmeyer, Bersani and Gagne, 2000)?

One strategy that can significantly enhance the achievement and maintenance of self-determined lifestyles for people with high and complex needs has been described under the rubric of person-centered planning. This approach emphasizes the input of the individual who is receiving support and those who know him or her well, in order to understand preferences, abilities, lifestyle choices, dreams and needs (Holburn and Vietze, 2002; Jackson and Panyan, 2002; Pearpoint, Forest and O'Brien, 1996; Vandercook, York and Forest, 1989). Perhaps most importantly, a focus on the perspectives, strengths and hopes of the individual informs a vision and plan for the future, information that can very happily be incorporated within the broader framework of positive behavior support (Carr et al., 2002; also see the case studies provided by Artesani and Mallar, 1998; and Magito-McLaughlin et al., 2002).

Ethical issues in the treatment of challenging behaviors

As we noted at the beginning of this chapter, quality of life factors and ethical approaches are best considered together in any plan to reduce or prevent challenging behaviors in people with developmental disabilities. Put simply, a concern to achieve an optimal quality of life, guided by principles of ethical and responsible action, underpins all of our efforts at assessment and intervention. This means that any support provided must be socially just, evidence-based, reflect a proper duty of care, acknowledge and build upon collaborative input, be responsible and morally defensible. Importantly, as we saw earlier, an individualized focus is imperative if we are to tailor and modify interventions following best practice guidelines. A little later, we will consider protocols that can be applied prior to, during and following episodes of challenging behavior as part of the positive behavior support process.

Without doubt, the use of aversive techniques in behavior change programs has triggered extensive debate. A vast literature has emerged in the past 10–15 years, centered on arguments for and against the use of aversive stimuli in various situations, including educational and residential programs. Alberto and Troutman (1999) noted that it is not so much the issue of effectiveness that raises a question mark in people's minds, rather, it is the appropriateness of using potentially intrusive approaches in terms of broader human and social rights (p. 309).

Emerson (1995) articulated this tension by recognizing the need to reconcile the unacceptability of using aversive methods with the potential for permanent damage that a person who engages in challenging behaviors such as self-injury or aggression may sustain or inflict. To this end, he argues that risk assessments represent an important pro-active strategy for personnel and systems involved in supporting individuals who demonstrate challenging behaviors, if the use of aversive procedures is being considered. That is, one must assess the risks of injury and if these are great, the use of more intrusive treatments may be justified.

During the past few decades, a number of prominent writers in this field have explored the concept of the right to effective treatment. Van Houten et al. (1988), for example, published a statement of principles to inform the use of behavioral strategies in the treatment of challenging behavior. These principles included the right to a therapeutic environment, the central importance of teaching functional skills within a framework of concern for the welfare of the person for whom behavior change is targeted, the involvement of appropriately qualified and experienced applied behavior analysts, the right to behavioral assessment and ongoing evaluation and perhaps most importantly, the right to access the most effective treatment available.

If we explore these principles a little further, it can be argued that there may be occasions when the use of a positive approach in and of itself is not effective, is less efficient than one involving more restrictive approaches, or that the time that elapses before changes are observed increases the seriousness or extent of risk to the person demonstrating challenging behaviors (Van Houten et al., 1988). From a duty of care perspective, a decision to forgo the introduction of what is considered to be a more restrictive practice may represent a breach of responsibility on the part of the clinician. In other words, to fail in the provision of effective techniques when other approaches have not worked could be judged to be unethical. As Van Houten et al. (1988) noted, 'in some cases, a client's right to effective treatment may dictate the immediate use of quicker acting, but temporarily more restrictive, procedures' (p. 383). These procedures may include stimuli considered to be aversive, if the use of such procedures has been empirically validated.

The delivery of an aversive stimulus can serve two functions: to reduce behavior (punishment) or to increase behavior when removed (negative reinforcement) (Alberto and Troutman, 1999). It should be noted that both processes, and especially negative reinforcement, can occur inadvertently. For example, an unplanned event such as peer attention may be perceived by one recipient as punishing and by another person as positively reinforcing. Conversely, removal of a difficult task due to the tantrums of the person expected to complete the work may operate to actually negatively reinforce (increase the possibility of) the antisocial behavior in the future (for a valuable discussion of this issue, see Maag, 2001).

Aversive events can be unconditioned, meaning that the recipient does not need a learning history to consider them unpleasant or punishing. Examples of unconditioned aversive stimuli include physical control (such as restraint), the presentation of unpleasant sensory experiences (smells, finely sprayed water on the face) and any pain-inducing experience, such as being hit or pinched. Conditioned aversive stimuli, on the other hand, are judged to be unpleasant by the recipient due to some association with an unconditioned aversive. Being yelled at is an example of a conditioned aversive and may be linked with the experience of a smack, hence yelling has a potential impact upon behavior (Alberto and Troutman, 1999).

In a timely paper, Singer, Gert and Koegel (1999) presented a moral framework to assist in discussion around the acceptability or otherwise of aversive procedures. They pointed out that harm arising from the delivery of punishers can involve the loss of pleasure, ability and freedom, as well as the experience of pain, with dehumanizing implications (p. 89) and potentially negative side-effects (Emerson, 1995). Singer et al. centered their analysis on the issues of who is a moral agent, who should be protected by moral rules and the question of whether there are occasions when the need to address problem behaviors justifies breaking the generally accepted moral code. With regard to the last point, it is critical to note their conclusion: "A growing body of empirical evidence indicates that there are nonaversive alternatives for addressing even the most serious behavior problems in people with severe cognitive disabilities" (1999, pp. 92–3). These alternatives, including positive behavior support and functional communication training are amply represented throughout this book. In this chapter, we focus upon several guiding principles derived from the literature that inform the selection of approaches that are non-intrusive, positive and ethically sound.

The first such principle reflects the importance of a socially just and positivist approach to behavior support, grounded in the dignity and needs of the individual and the broader contexts in which they live (Carr et al., 2002; Jackson and Panyan, 2002). Rather than utilizing punishment to reduce behavior, the educator or service provider focuses on the ability of the individual and promotes participation and access in order to build on existing skills and prevent or reduce opportunities for antisocial behavior. Indeed, Carr et al. (2002) note that:

> the best time to intervene on problem behavior is when the behavior is not occurring. Intervention takes place in the absence of problem behavior so that such behavior can be prevented from occurring again. The proactive nature of PBS [*positive behavior support*] stands in sharp contrast to traditional approaches, which have emphasized the use of aversive procedures that address problem behaviors with reactive, crisis-driven strategies ... (p. 9, italics added)

A second theme extends upon this concept by highlighting the role of a considered and minimalist approach if it is not possible to avoid the use of aversive strategies altogether. In other words, are there strategies that are less intrusive that can be introduced, to achieve the same goal? Are they part of a pre-conceived plan that is morally and ethically sound? One test of the moral acceptability of any given aversive technique has been provided by Jackson and Panyan (2002): 'Would we find this technique offensive if it was to be used on us? If so, why are people with disabilities any different (p. 74)?'

Vittimberga, Scotti and Weigle (1999) have argued that although there is little empirical evidence to indicate that a least to most hierarchy of intrusiveness is always followed in practice, there are sound reasons for the adoption of such an approach (p. 58). Their rationale focuses on the central importance of an educative model of intervention and support in which skills and adaptive progression contrast with the simple reduction of inappropriate behaviors and the absence of supportive, functional and generalization-friendly environments.

Implications for service delivery and practice

Teachers, parents, caregivers and others interacting with individuals who display challenging behaviors invariably work as part of a team or family structure. One way of conceptualizing the work of this team is to consider the nature of intervention and assistance within a continuum of broad to specific practices. As we have noted, positive behavior support is a process that aims to facilitate support. That support may range from interventions to reduce specific behaviors to gathering community and cultural accommodations around the individual (Horner, 2000). The central advantage of this comprehensive and ecologically sound model is the potential for generalized and sustained shifts in the repertoire of individuals and the contexts in which they function. Of course, the integration of PBS elements into a cohesive plan that is meaningful at an individual level is a complex process, with many ramifications for professional development and collaborative teaming.

Another useful means of conceptualizing the delivery of support is linear in nature, involving the evaluation of issues in the prevention or reduction of challenging behavior before, during and after the development of a formal support plan or a particular behavioral episode. In Table 4.1, we have listed a series of protocols that can be used to inform the planning process, without specifying a particular phase (before, during, after). As you read them, it may be valuable to consider their place in a systemic and systematic approach to behavior support. What are their bases in the quality of life and ethics literature that we have reviewed, and at what point (or points) in the development of positive behavior supports could (or should!) these questions be asked?

Table 4.1 Quality of life and ethical considerations for program design

1. How involved in behavior support planning is the person exhibiting challenging behaviors?
   a. opportunities for self-advocacy?
   b. indicators of choice, communication and control of life events?

2. In any given day, how many people, places and activities are available to the person for whom the intervention is designed?
   a. to what degree do these experiences reflect the preferences of the individual?

3. What guidelines exist within the state, district and organization in relation to the management of challenging behavior, and are they followed scrupulously?

4. Within the support plan, is there evidence of measurable goals for skill development as well as behavior reduction targets?

5. If there is a plan for the use of aversive stimuli;
   a. has a risk assessment been conducted and if so, what were the findings?
   b. have strategies that are more positive and less intrusive been systematically trialed and evaluated?
   c. is there a simultaneous focus upon skill development as well as behavior reduction?
   d. is a system of least to most intrusive approaches planned, with effectiveness data collected and monitored?

6. What plans are in place for generalized behavior support across people, places, times and activities?

7. Are there professional development needs to be identified and addressed with personnel involved in the provision of behavior support?

As Table 4.1 illustrates, there are many questions we can ask of our practices before, during and following the process of positive behavior support or a specific incident. From a preventative point of view, the issues of lifestyle options, genuine participation opportunities, preference identification, choices and control can be highlighted. Pro-actively, the importance of a crisis plan cannot be overstated, and invariably such an initiative will be informed by systematic data collection and analysis (see Chapter 6). Clearly, the collection of information that allows support personnel to predict the occurrence of problem behaviors (for example, broad setting events or specific antecedents), can be used to make accommodations wherever possible. However, this will not always be successful and incidents will still occur. Jackson and Panyan (2002) have provided a valuable discussion of various strategies for use when an individual is in a crisis cycle (Walker, Colvin and Ramsey, 1995). Having a plan in advance (as opposed to an immediate unconsidered reaction) is important. As part of the plan, clinicians should specify the desired outcomes and develop hypotheses as to the cause of the behavior (Jackson and Panyan, 2002).

The actual demonstration of challenging behavior brings with it a number of ethical issues, as discussed above, centered upon the use of moral and responsible approaches, a right to treatment and the duty of care shared by educators and other support-providers. Three issues will be discussed here. First, the importance of carefully and fully reconciling daily management practices with the plans approved by the service provider and consented to by parents and other relevant stakeholders. In this context, open lines of communication as well as collaborative and transparent support practices are critical. Second, selection of the least intrusive strategy and implementation in a manner that ensures the safety of the supported individual (Jackson and Panyan, 2002).

Third, there is a need for systematic collection of data to evaluate the effectiveness and appropriateness of intervention strategies. A related issue here is the scheduling of time to sit down and evaluate the data, potentially leading to program modification and changed routines and practices, including the behavior of support personnel. If a strategy that is judged to be quite intrusive upon personal freedom (such as brief restraint) is used regularly and as a matter of course, a review of practice guidelines will probably be necessary, with a view to the selection of more positive, less punitive options.

Finally, an ethical approach to behavior support involves an ongoing commitment to maximizing quality of life, especially by enhancing opportunities for self-determination and regulation. It is no longer acceptable to simply target and reduce problem behavior, without attending to a vision for individualized lifestyle choices and community membership. Accordingly, planning must reflect the ongoing input of the person for whom support is intended, or their advocate, and a systematic approach to the achievement of independent and generalized social participation in the long term.

Summary and conclusion

In this chapter we have reviewed the complex issues surrounding quality of life and ethical considerations in the provision of support to reduce or prevent challenging behavior. As we have noted, this is not a simple or discrete area. We spent quite a bit of time considering legal, moral and practical aspects in the provision of positive behavior support and examining the ways in which these factors combine in the ecology of an individual, a school or a system. Duty of care, least intrusive options and morally responsible perspectives were reviewed in our discussion of the aversives debate, setting the scene for consideration of assessment and screening practices and the design of individually appropriate positive intervention plans in the following chapters.

PART 3

ASSESSMENT OF CHALLENGING BEHAVIOR

CHAPTER 5

Health and medical screening

Introduction

Few would argue with the sentiment that being healthy is a good thing. Health and wellness are important to one's quality of life (Cummins, 1991; Parmenter, 1994). Good health increases longevity and is a necessary prerequisite to participation in many aspects of daily life. Poor health can be a major handicap whether or not one has a developmental disability. In addition to their influence on quality of life, health and medical issues can also affect learning, development and behavior; just as learning, development and behavior can affect health and wellness.

For a variety of reasons individuals with developmental disabilities are generally less healthy and more susceptible to certain medical and mental health problems than people without disabilities (Evenhuis et al., 2001). Strategies to promote health are therefore of considerable importance, but effective strategies to promote health are all too often absent in developmental disability services (Carlson, 2002).

There is another reason to promote health and well-being in persons with developmental disabilities and that is because medical conditions can influence challenging behavior in various and complex ways, as was briefly discussed in Chapter 2. This chapter extends that prior discussion by considering the influence of health and medical issues on challenging behaviors in people with developmental disabilities and the resultant need for health promotion and medical screening in the treatment of challenging behavior. In doing so, we will consider the general health and medical issues that arise in developmental disabilities and delineate some of the mechanisms by which health issues and medical conditions might influence challenging behavior.

The evidence reviewed in this chapter supports a view that medical conditions can and often do play a role in the emergence and maintenance of challenging behavior. That medical conditions can play a role in the emergence and maintenance of challenging behavior does not mean that they always do so, but it does mean that there will often be a need for medical screening and specialist medical supports in the treatment of challenging behaviors.

While the emergence of a challenging behavior might be attributed to some medical condition in some cases, the theory of challenging behavior outlined in Chapter 3 states that once challenging behavior occurs it will be shaped by its consequences and thus all interventions must consider how consequences have shaped the behavior and what consequences are maintaining the behavior. Clinicians must consider the interaction of medical and biological factors with operant learning mechanisms in the emergence and maintenance of challenging behavior. Such considerations are also necessary in developing effective interventions to prevent and reduce challenging behavior (see Chapter 8).

In addition to links with the more general theory of Chapter 3, two ethical principles that are consistent with the issues discussed in Chapter 4 underlie this chapter. The first is to do no harm. With all treatments, it is critical to ensure that the intervention procedures do not cause more problems than the problem behavior being treated. With some treatments, the harm may be long deferred but the potential for harm must nonetheless be considered. For example, psychotropic medications might be indicated because of a diagnosis of major mental illness, but prolonged use of some neuroleptic medications can cause serious and irreversible side-effects. Additional interventions must therefore be explored so that medication use, if and when it is indicated, is neither prolonged nor used at the larger dosages that increase the risk of developing serious and permanent side-effects.

The second ethical principle is the right to effective treatment (Van Houten et al., 1988) as discussed in Chapter 4. The right to effective treatment implies to us that challenging behavior must be addressed with active and empirically validated procedures, rather than simply being dismissed, accepted or tolerated. All too often early signs of challenging behavior are dismissed in the mistaken hope that the child will grow out of it (see Chapter 8). Unfortunately, once challenging behaviors appear in the repertoires of persons with developmental disabilities they tend to persist and get worse over time. Early and active treatment is indicated. Treatment must be responsive and if the first treatment tried is not effective, then clinicians must be willing to turn to other evidence-based procedures. No advocate would seriously consider allowing a person to suffer with a treatable illness or infection and so no advocate should allow a person to persist with challenging behaviors when effective treatments are available. There is no dignity in allowing challenging behavior to persist for the clinician, the family, or the individual with the developmental disability. This is often done under the guise of benevolence. All too often the guise prevents the development of systematic data-driven interventions.

There is merit in a systematic approach to developing and implementing interventions to reduce challenging behaviors. There is now growing evidence that comprehensive behavioral support for individuals with developmental disabilities and challenging behavior must include a consideration of health and medical issues, including screening for mental health problems. In this chapter we hope to reveal the merit of addressing and assessing health and medical issues as part of a systematic approach to developing effective interventions.

Health and medical problems

No one is healthy all the time, but illnesses, infections, diseases, and injuries afflict some people more often and more seriously than others. Among the most vulnerable are people with developmental disabilities. As noted in Chapter 2, compared with their peers without disabilities, individuals with developmental disabilities – particularly those with the most severe, multiple disabilities – tend to be less healthy and more prone to illness, infection, and injury than their non-handicapped peers (Dunne, Asher and Rivara, 1993; Evenhuis et al., 2001; Lennox et al., 2000; Orelove and Sobsey, 1996).

These differences in health status between persons with and without developmental disabilities are often large. Indeed, the international research literature points to major deficiencies in the health status of people with developmental disabilities (Lennox et al., 2001). Some of the more common health care problems seen in developmental disability clinics include communicable diseases (e.g. colds, flu, hepatitis, parasitic infections), dual diagnosis (e.g. intellectual disability plus depression), infections of the ear, bladder and urinary tract, as well as a range of complex problems arising from seizure disorders.

Obviously some of these conditions and other common illnesses and injuries do not only affect people with developmental disabilities. The general findings of increased health problems relative to the general population should not, therefore, be taken to mean that disease, poor health, and increased rates of psychiatric diagnoses, injuries and illnesses are inevitable just because someone has a developmental disability. Indeed, Matt Janicki and his colleagues (Janicki et al., 2002) found that one group of 1,371 adults with intellectual disabilities (aged 40–79 years) were characterized as being in good health, contrary to what international trends would lead one to expect. This positive finding could reflect a cohort effect in that the current generation might be healthier due to improved living conditions and medical care. On the other hand, it could also be that certain health problems went undetected in the cohort studied by Janicki et al. Despite pockets of good health, the literature overall suggests that there will be more health problems and injuries among people with developmental disabilities and this implies the need for medical care that is capable of maintaining health and wellness in a vulnerable population.

There are several probable reasons for the higher prevalence of health and medical concerns among individuals with developmental disabilities. Some of the reasons, discussed next, could be conceptualized in terms of the characteristics shared by people with developmental disabilities, which distinguish them from people without disabilities as discussed in Chapter 1.

First, some developmental disability syndromes and certain conditions associated with various syndromes (e.g. seizures, skeletal deformities, vision and hearing impairment) may increase one's susceptibility to injury, illness, and infection. Consider the following examples:

- A person with poor mobility and vision is more prone to injuries from falling, and walking into objects.
- Complex seizure disorders are reported in a significant percentage of people with developmental disabilities (nearly 80% of people with severe/multiple disabilities), which is itself a major health concern (Sobsey and Thuppal, 1996).
- Children with Down syndrome, as noted by Sobsey and Thuppal (1996), appear particularly susceptible to respiratory infections and, once infected, they may suffer more severe symptoms.

Second, the lifestyles and living conditions of people with developmental disabilities may reduce their resistance to illness and increase their susceptibility to infection and injury. Contributing lifestyle factors include poor diet, lack of exercise and congregate living conditions associated with larger residential facilities. Calcium, vitamin D and exercise, for example, are necessary for healthy bones, but people with developmental disabilities may receive insufficient amounts of all three of these essential ingredients (Tohill, 1997). This may, in turn, lead to increased bone fractures from falls that might otherwise have been inconsequential. Medications for seizures may also increase susceptibility to bone fractures by decreasing bone density (Tohill, 1997). Unbelievable as it may sound, a fractured bone can go undetected in cases where the person cannot communicate their pain (Gunsett et al., 1989), but the pain is no less real and it is not inconceivable that this pain would cause irritability and increase challenging behavior.

Tohill and Laverty (2001) explained the need for behavioral medicine programs to improve health. In particular, they recommended a behavioral intervention focused on lifestyle changes to ensure that individuals with developmental disabilities receive the recommended daily amount of calcium and vitamin D in their diet as well as receive some (safe) level of exposure to sunlight, which is a source of vitamin D. Intervention may also often be needed to establish an exercise routine that is compatible with the person's physical capabilities. Along this later line, aerobic exercise may not only improve bone density, but might also improve intellectual functioning and self-concept (Gabler-Halle, Halle and Chung, 1993). As part of the overall care, seizure medications and indeed all medications, must be monitored on a regular basis to ensure the lowest possible effective dose is being used, as this may vary tremendously from person to person.

Third, deficits in adaptive behavior functioning may increase vulnerability to illness and injury. Deficits in self-care skills such as washing, feeding and toileting increase the risk of exposure to viruses and bacteria that may cause illness. Hygiene is important, but our experience suggests it is often neglected in residential, vocational and educational programs for individuals with developmental disabilities. Too often the habilitation and educational programs fail to include goals to develop independence in self-care skills that would promote greater hygienic practices. Too often the home, workplace, or classroom is not maintained with an eye to eliminating unhygienic conditions.

Fourth, most people with developmental disabilities will have substantial deficits in communication ability. Deficits in expressive language will make it difficult if not impossible for the person to alert others when they start to feel unwell. This will likely mean that early symptoms go undetected. Treatment will therefore be delayed until the symptoms become more obvious. This is a major problem. Symptoms typically become more obvious when the illness is more severe, which makes treatment just that much more difficult. It also creates a larger window of opportunity for the individual to discover, and for others in the environment to reinforce, coping responses; which, for those with highly restricted repertoires, may take the form of challenging behavior. In addition, expressive language problems will make it difficult for the person to describe their symptoms accurately, which will again no doubt hinder treatment.

Deficits in receptive speech or the comprehension of language will also affect medical treatment. The person may be unable to comprehend medical instructions or follow the prescription accurately. There is an obvious need for programming to develop communication skills related to health and medical issues, but communication intervention programs for individuals with developmental disabilities have not yet provided empirically validated procedures for teaching these types of communication skills (Sigafoos, 1997).

Combine all of these four probabilities with the fact that most medical practitioners and psychiatrists appear to have little specialist knowledge of and experience with developmental disabilities and it becomes clear why providing good medical care is difficult. In the hands of an untrained and inexperienced practitioner, satisfactory resolution of the person's health and medical problems would seem a rather long shot. In a series of studies, Nick Lennox and his colleagues have documented the lack of knowledge and experience in developmental disabilities among medical practitioners (Lennox and Diggens, 1999a; Lennox et al., 2000; Lennox et al., 2001). This program of research has involved surveys of medical practitioners regarding their training and experience in treating individuals with developmental disabilities. In one representative study, Lennox and Diggens (1999b) conducted telephone interviews with staff at Australian medical schools. The aim of these interviews was to determine the amount and nature of training provided to medical students on the health care of people with intellectual disabilities. The results tell a familiar story. Overall, there was a general lack of systematic and comprehensive training in this area, although the amount of training differed widely from school to school. Medical practitioners themselves report feelings of being unprepared due to lack of training, and having little experience with developmentally disabled patients. This holds whether one interviews general practitioners (Lennox, Diggens and Ugoni, 1997) or psychiatrists (Lennox and Chaplin, 1995).

Given the relative lack of health and medical expertise, it may often be difficult to obtain a thorough health and medical screening to assess the influence of such factors on challenging behavior (Lennox and Chaplin, 1996). Clinicians must therefore become more aware of how health and medical problems can influence challenging behavior so that they will be in a better position to support medical practitioners in undertaking health and medical screening of persons with developmental disabilities.

Mental health

Although mental health aspects of developmental disability could be subsumed under the more general health and medical issues covered so far in this chapter, there is enough here that is unique to warrant a separate section. We acknowledge that even this is inadequate. Unfortunately, we can only hope to provide a bare minimum of information on psychopathology in persons with developmental disabilities for two reasons. First, a single chapter could never do this important topic justice and second, we do not have the required expertise. Fortunately, entire volumes have been written on psychopathology in persons with developmental disabilities (Matson and Barrett, 1993) and there is even now an entire journal devoted to this topic (*Mental Health Aspects of Developmental Disabilities*). Readers are therefore urged to consult these sources.

As noted in Chapter 2, there is evidence that people with developmental disabilities can experience the full range of psychiatric disorders found in the general population. In fact, persons with developmental disabilities have a high prevalence of psychiatric disorders; a combination that is known as dual diagnosis (see Reber and Borcherding, 1997 for a review). There is also little doubt that psychiatric disorders such as depression and anxiety disorders can influence challenging behaviors. Indeed, diagnostic criteria for certain psychiatric disorders often make explicit reference to challenging behaviors. A sudden increase in aggression or self-injury, for example, is a possible symptom of major depression for children with mental retardation. Severe tantrums could, in some cases, be viewed as the manifestation of inappropriate emotional expression associated with schizophrenia (Reber and Borcherding, 1997).

Still, it is often unclear if the effect of a psychiatric disorder on challenging behavior is direct or indirect, as discussed in Chapter 2. In cases where a psychiatric disorder appears later in the life of a person with developmental disability, say during adolescence, it may be possible to attribute the collateral appearance of challenging behavior to the direct effects of a psychiatric disorder. Indicators of an emerging psychiatric disorder include changes in the person's typical behavioral patterns, such as changes in appetite, sleeping patterns and social interaction. Alternatively, if there had been a history of challenging behavior prior to the emergence of mental illness, then any collateral increase may represent the indirect effects of the psychiatric condition. In either case the disordered behavior will make contact with environmental contingencies that will, in turn, shape the behavior. For example, an episode of mania may increase the probability of aggression but only when the person is restricted from engaging in some (manic) activity. Similarly, depression may be indicated by increased time spent sleeping and the person may thus react with tantrums when others attempt to get the person out of bed to perform what would otherwise be easily tolerated and reasonable requirements, such as showering, dressing and sitting down to breakfast.

A related issue is whether the person's developmental disability is primary or secondary to the mental illness. Along these lines, it may be difficult if not impossible to determine whether the person's challenging behaviors are primarily related to the developmental disability or instead represent the manifestation of psychiatric disturbance (Reiss, 1993). Given the difficulty of making such distinctions, there will be a need to assess factors that could be influencing challenging behavior and a comprehensive assessment along these lines will require a thorough psychiatric screening.

The psychiatrist John Hillery (1999) noted that the relation between challenging behavior and mental illness might be conceptualized as either primary, secondary, or consequential. An example of a primary relation would be that the challenging behavior is a sign or symptom of the mental illness. In contrast a secondary relation would be something such as having a panic attack, which establishes escape from that situation as a reinforcer and therefore increases the probability of any behaviors that have enabled the person to escape. So if a student panics and attempts to leave the classroom, and if the teacher stops the student from leaving, then the student might respond with aggression. In a consequential relation, challenging behavior may occur as a symptom, but gets inadvertently reinforced and is therefore shaped into an operant behavior. It is probably this mechanism that accounts for how some people with seizure disorders learn to fake a seizure so as to obtain attention or escape from non-preferred activities.

It is often difficult to determine in cases of dual diagnosis, whether any given challenging behavior is primary, secondary or consequential. Part of the problem stems from the fact that screening for psychopathology is more difficult when the person has a developmental disability. Part of the difficulty is that psychiatric symptoms found in the general population may not manifest in the same way in people with developmental disabilities. Diagnostic criteria for numerous conditions (e.g. depression, anxiety, schizophrenia) are contained in the fourth edition of the *Diagnostic and Statistical Manual of Mental Disorders* (DSM-IV) published by the American Psychiatric Association (1994). Thompson, Axtell and Schaal (1993) highlighted the arguable assumptions that are made in adopting these criteria for diagnosing psychopathology in people with developmental disabilities:

> Many clinicians assume signs of mental illness in people with mental retardation are the same as those in nondisabled people, and that it is possible to extrapolate from these signs and symptoms, combined with patient and family histories, to arrive at a valid diagnosis. (p. 185)

Thompson et al. went on to note that there is little empirical evidence to make such assumptions. Clearly much more needs to be learnt about the manifestation of mental illnesses in people with developmental disabilities.

At present, it is important to consider the possibility that people with developmental disabilities who have a mental illness may not necessarily exhibit the same symptoms as non-disabled people. In addition, diagnostic signs that seemingly indicate a psychiatric disorder may not necessarily indicate the presence of a mental illness. In the later case, if the person also exhibits challenging behavior, then there is the danger that the signs will lead to a psychiatric diagnosis (e.g. depression) when none exists and then this (mis)diagnosis will be used to justify a pharmacological treatment (e.g. anti-depressants) that may be neither necessary nor effective.

On the other hand, there is the danger that a psychiatric disorder may be present, but go unrecognized because the symptoms, including perhaps increased challenging behavior, are not consistent with DSM-IV criteria. Here the symptoms might be simply attributed to the developmental disability with no attempt made to address the underlying psychiatric disorder.

Overall it is difficult to know the extent to which challenging behaviors in people with developmental disabilities are related to or influenced by psychopathology. Psychiatric disorders certainly affect a significant percentage of people with developmental disabilities (Matson and Barrett, 1993) and it is hard to imagine that such conditions would not influence challenging behavior in some important ways. In fact, based on the extensive use of psychotropic medications in this population, at least in some settings, one would have to assume that mental illness is rife, at least as rife as challenging behaviors. In some surveys of medication use, it has been found that a significant percentage of people with challenging behavior receive psychotropic medications for challenging behaviors even when they do not have a psychiatric disorder (Aman, Sarphare and Burrow, 1995; Sigafoos et al., 1994). Thus, extensive use of psychotropic medications does not necessarily equate to a correspondingly extensive prevalence of psychiatric disorders nor does it indicate a psychiatric basis for the person's challenging behaviors. Instead, it could mean that psychotropic medications are often prescribed for behavioral control in cases where there is no psychiatric diagnosis to justify the use of medication (Young and Hawkins, 2002).

The use of a psychotropic medication for behavioral control, in the absence of a psychiatric diagnosis to justify the use of that medication, is inappropriate. Such medications (e.g. antipsychotics, anxiolytics, anti-depressants) can have serious and irreversible side effects, as mentioned before. In the long term, prolonged use of such medications may cause more harm than good.

Even in short-term behavioral control, the use of psychotropic medications is questionable. Instead of suppressing behavioral problems some medications may have the exact opposite effect of increasing and exacerbating challenging behaviors in some individuals. Additionally, we have often heard that the use of such medication to control challenging behavior is justified because it might calm (sedate) the person and this will create a window of opportunity for clinicians to develop and implement behavioral and educational interventions. Once the behavioral or educational intervention kicks in, then the person can be gradually weaned from the medication, or so the story goes. From our clinical experiences, this almost never happens. Instead it seems that medications are used in lieu of developing a better lifestyle for the person and in lieu of good behavioral and educational programming. Even if the intentions for medication administration are good, some medications can make the person so lethargic and unresponsive that even the best behavioral or educational treatments are unlikely to have any positive effect. It is hard to teach communication skills, for example, to an individual who is so sedated by antipsychotic medication that they're half asleep for most of the day. If there ever was a single most important prerequisite for learning, being awake must surely be it.

Another problem with psychotropic medications is that they are not specific to challenging behavior in the sense of selectively suppressing challenging behaviors alone. A psychotropic medication might suppress challenging behaviors, but this does not mean that it suppresses only challenging behavior. Instead, the entire repertoire might be suppressed, including whatever few adaptive behaviors the person may have acquired.

It is overly optimistic to think that medication alone will solve the complex processes that lead to the emergence and persistence of challenging behavior in persons with developmental disabilities. While the use of medications can be justified in certain cases, such as when there is a clear indication of psychiatric disorder, it is worth repeating that the use of psychotropic medications for the treatment of challenging behaviors in the absence of any psychiatric indication is difficult to justify.

Even when there may be some justification, there is limited evidence to support the effectiveness of psychotropic medications for the treatment of challenging behavior in people with developmental disabilities. Following an impressive review of the literature on this issue, Kennedy and Meyer (1998) concluded that: "Currently researchers cannot demonstrate whether most drugs prescribed to reduce challenging behavior are effective or predict when adverse side effects will emerge from their use" (p. 83). This conclusion is consistent with guidelines offered by Kerbeshian, Burd and Avery (2001) who noted that: "Use of medications must be guided by an awareness of habilitative, behavioral, social, administrative, and ethical issues" (p. 199). Awareness of medical problems, including mental health issues, is critical to understanding challenging behavior and to the provision of effective support to individuals with developmental disabilities and challenging behaviors.

Medical problems and challenging behavior

Medical problems have long been indicated as possible contributors to challenging behavior and not just in people with developmental disabilities. A classic report on this issue was published in 1963 in *The Journal of Genetic Psychology*. In this report, Vladimir De Lissovoy from the Pennsylvania State University's Department of Child Development and Family relations compared 15 children who engaged in head banging with a matched sample of 15 similarly aged children with no history of head banging. The two groups were of similar age (10–42 months), IQ (mean of 109.2 and 113.8), and gender composition (i.e. 11 boys and 4 girls). The children did not have disabilities. What differed for the two groups of children was their respective medical histories. Specifically, six of the children who engaged in head banging had a history of ear infection (otitis media) within the first year of life. Only one of the non-head-banging children had a history of ear infection. This difference, which was statistically significant, suggests that otitis media may precipitate the emergence of head banging in otherwise typically developing infants and children.

In fact in four of the six cases, otitis media preceded the onset of head banging, as would be required if the ear infection caused head banging. In addition, children with recurrent ear infections had more severe head banging, which further suggests some causal relation. In his articulate discussion of these findings, De Lissovoy discussed mechanisms that could account for this association that goes something like this: The pain of an ear infection is no doubt distressing for the child. This may therefore increase agitation and the child might, in agitation, accidentally bang his or her head against the crib. If head banging offers some temporary relief or distraction from the pain of the ear infection, then one can see how head banging could be shaped into an operant response maintained by its (negatively) reinforcing consequences (e.g. distraction from pain and temporary pain relief).

Given the early date of De Lissovoy's study, it is surprising that relatively little subsequent research has taken heed of his findings. The link between medical conditions and challenging behavior in persons with developmental disabilities seems rarely to be explored either in the archival literature or in clinical practice. It is difficult to know whether this is because such links are rare or rarely examined.

One relevant study appeared in the *Journal of Autism and Developmental Disorders* (Gunsett et al., 1989). To introduce their research, the team noted that the limited verbal repertoires of individuals with developmental disabilities may precipitate the emergence of challenging behavior "when there is a need to communicate physical distress" (p. 168). They also noted that clinicians: "face some degree of pressure to provide immediate [educational and behavioral] treatment, and not to insist on thorough medical investigation before providing an intervention which might mask medical etiology" (p. 168). As these two quotes suggest, Gunsett et al. were proposing that in some cases challenging behaviors may be an attempt to communicate a physical illness or injury. The results of their investigation of severely to profoundly disabled residents in a large facility provide some support for this proposition.

In this study, Gunsett et al. (1989) reported on the results of annual physical examinations of 56 people who had been referred for treatment because of challenging behavior. In 13 of these 56 individuals, it was determined that their challenging behaviors could have a medical cause. Following a thorough medical screening, 10 of the 13 were shown to have medical conditions that were likely influencing challenging behavior. Various medical diagnoses were made. For example, one individual had a compound fracture in her leg, two clients had urinary tract infections, one had an impacted bowel, and another had a toxic level of anticonvulsant medication in her blood stream.

The next phase of their study involved aggressive treatment of the identified medical problem. To assess the effects of medical treatment on challenging behavior, ratings were made to ascertain whether the various problem behaviors (e.g. screaming, biting, head banging, aggression) were the same, better or worse following medical treatment. The results were that one client's challenging behavior was rated as worse and one as the same, but for the remaining eight individuals, challenging behaviors were rated as better. These data highlight the importance of regular and thorough medical screenings, especially when the individual presents with challenging behavior. The data also indicate a critical need to develop communication skills that will enable the individual to inform others when they are ill and in pain. As mentioned before communication intervention programs for individuals with developmental disabilities have neglected these types of communication skills (Sigafoos, 1997).

Another more recent study (Bosch et al., 1997) looked at medical histories of persons with severe mental retardation who had histories of self-injurious behaviors such as head banging and hand mouthing. These researchers had noticed that several clients referred for behavioral treatment of self-injury were discovered to have previously unrecognized medical problems. The medical problems were of such severity that they were likely to have caused much pain and discomfort, which could exacerbate challenging behavior. To examine this hypothesis systematically, the researchers conducted a retrospective chart review of 25 developmentally disabled clients (3 to 35 years of age) referred for behavioral services. These 25 individuals were selected for review, because a prior experimental-functional analysis (see Chapter 7) could not identify an operant function for the behavior. The authors argue that this negative result could signal that the behavior is being influenced by a medical problem. Their review of these 25 cases turned up seven patients with undiagnosed medical conditions. As with Gunsett et al. (1989) various medical diagnoses were made (e.g. otitis media, constipation, duodenal ulcer, rhinitis). With medical treatment, self-injury decreased for six of these seven clients.

Considered together, these three studies (Bosch et al., 1997; De Lissovoy, 1963; Gunsett et al., 1989) are highly suggestive of a role of medical conditions in the emergence and exacerbation of challenging behavior. However, these studies are limited due to lack of experimental control and small sample sizes. Still, despite limitations in the research methodology, there is little doubt among professionals that medical conditions can precipitate and exacerbate challenging behavior and little doubt that a thorough medical screening is an indispensable component of the assessment and treatment of challenging behavior.

Screening

Now that we have seen examples of the types of medical problems that may contribute to challenging behavior and considered how health and medical problems might precipitate the emergence, persistence, and exacerbation of challenging behavior, we must consider how to assess the influence of such factors for any given individual. The prior review provides an idea of the types of medical problems to look for. At a minimum, a clinician can alert medical doctors, who may be untrained and inexperienced in this area, to look for these types of problems. Beyond the minimum, a thorough medical screening involves consideration of the factors listed in Table 5.1.

In screening for health and medical conditions, there is a need to consider whether the influence of a medical condition is direct or indirect. Direct means the medical condition is the primary reason why the behavior occurs. In such cases medical treatment may be sufficient to resolve the challenging behavior. In other cases, however, challenging behaviors, even though they may have a medical etiology, may nonetheless require an integration of medical and behavioral/education treatments. Recall the Carr and McDowell (1980) study described in Chapter 2 in which a 10-year-old boy began scratching in response to dermatitis. Once started, however, the behavior was shaped by prevailing contingencies and acquired an operant function. Also mentioned in Chapter 2, was the possibility that medical conditions may act as a setting event or establishing operation for challenging behavior. A child with a head cold, an upset

Table 5.1 Factors to consider in health and medical screening

Factor	Consideration
Environment	• Is the environment clean and appropriately maintained? • Is there good temperature control? • Is the environment free of hazards and toxins?
Lifestyle	• Does the person have good hygiene skills (e.g. washing, feeding, dental care, toileting)? • Is the diet balanced and nutritious? • Does the person take regular exercise? • Is there appropriate exposure to fresh air and sunshine? • Does the person smoke, drink alcohol or abuse drugs?
Mental health	• Does the person have a mental illness? • Could mental health problems be an acute reaction to environmental stress (e.g. death of family member, loss of previous skills)? • Is appropriate psychiatric care provided when necessary? • If psychotropic medications are used is their use justified and monitored at least once per month?
Health promotion	• Does the person receive regular medical examinations? • Does the person receive regular dental examinations? • Are efforts in place to teach hygienic skills, if absent? • Are efforts in place to promote healthy lifestyles (e.g. diet and exercise)? • Does the person have the means and skills to communicate pain, illness, and discomfort?
Medical care and screening	• Prior to or in conjunction with behavioral and educational assessment and intervention, has the individual received an examination covering vision, hearing, allergies, adverse reactions to medication, and unrecognized medical conditions that may be influencing challenging behavior? • Have any identified medical problems been resolved? • Are referrals to specialists made when necessary? • Can the individual and carers comply with required medical treatments?

stomach, or even a sore toe, for example, might react to practitioner requests with a tantrum because the illness has made her more irritable than usual. Thus, one useful approach might be to reduce the expectations and demands that are made of the child until they are feeling better.

When health and medical problems are the issue, one should expect the child's health-related behaviors to improve when the health and medical issues are resolved. That is, the behaviors are unlikely to remain acute if appropriate medical care is implemented early. However, if the challenging behavior is reinforced and if the person's repertoire has few alternative behaviors, then challenging behavior is likely to persist even when the medical issue has been resolved. Such cases will almost certainly require a more complex intervention plan involving ongoing medical, behavioral, educational, and more general lifestyle interventions (see Chapters 7 and 8).

Bio-behavioral states

In addition to screening (to rule out health and medical problems or to treat appropriately any problems that may be identified), it may also be important to assess bio-behavioral states. The idea here is that certain states might be associated with increased probability of challenging behavior and this information could be critical for developing educational and behavioral interventions.

Helm and Simeonsson (1989) defined behavioral states as "expressions of the maturity, status, and organization of the central nervous system. They mediate the person's ability to respond to the environment and stimulation" (p. 203). Examples of behavior states referred to in the literature include awake-active, awake-active (self-stimulatory), crying, dazed and drowsy.

Doug Guess and colleagues at the University of Kansas studied behavioral states in children with developmental disabilities (e.g. Guess et al., 1993). Their data revealed reliable patterns of behavioral states and showed that a range of external and organic factors, such as medication, diet and social interactions may influence behavior states. These findings would seem to have important implications for understanding challenging behaviors.

Along these lines, Reese (1997) observed a man with profound disability and a history of self-injurious behavior. First, Reese investigated the relation between behavior state and self-injury. Reese showed that self-injury varied depending on the prevailing behavioral state. For example, when alert, the man was less likely to demonstrate self-injury when engaged in an activity with other people. When he was rated as being non-alert, however, higher levels of self-injury were observed.

Second, Reese (1997) examined the effects of environmental programming and medication (Fluphenazine) on the man's self-injury. Treatment varied depending on whether the participant was judged to be alert or non-alert. Reese found that both intervention phases (environmental arrangement and environmental arrangement with medication) produced lower rates of self-injury when compared to a baseline phase with neither treatment in place. These results suggested that behavior states could influence challenging behaviors as well as the effectiveness of treatments. While these conclusions must be viewed as tentative owing to the limited number of studies on this topic, information on behavioral states should be considered because this type of data may enable clinicians to better understand changes in the probability of challenging behavior and this in turn may assist in selecting treatment strategies.

Summary and conclusion

In a preface to their book on instructional procedures, Duker, Didden and Sigafoos (in press) noted that

> The severity and hence the impact on learning of a developmental disability is a joint function of the cause or etiology of the condition, the degree of intellectual impairment, extent of adaptive behavior development, and if present, the frequency and severity of problem behavior. (p. iv)

To this quote we could add that the impact on learning, development, and behavior is also a function of the person's health status. It is no doubt the case that learning, development, and behavior also influence a person's health. If we are correct in this insight, then the implication for service delivery is clear. Services that aim to support individuals with developmental disability must include efforts to promote and maintain health, and services that aim to improve health must include efforts to develop healthy lifestyles and health-promoting behaviors.

Our review of the literature for this chapter indicates that interventions to improve and maintain health and wellness are relatively neglected in services for individuals with developmental disabilities. This is a major problem because individuals with developmental disabilities are – for a variety of reasons – highly susceptible to health and medical problems, including mental illness. Medical and psychiatric care is further compromised when doctors and psychiatrists have limited experience with and knowledge of developmental disability.

Existing data are highly suggestive that psychiatric disorders and medical conditions can greatly influence the emergence and persistence of challenging behavior. Numerous and various disorders and conditions have been implicated as having such a role, indicating the need for thorough and comprehensive psychiatric and medical screening in conjunction with behavioral and educational assessment and intervention. The mechanisms by which psychiatric and medical conditions might influence challenging behavior can be direct and/or indirect. This indicates the need for an integration of medical with behavioral/educational assessment and interventions, and with larger system-based interventions that are focused on improving quality of life through ecological and lifestyle changes. This need for an integrated approach means that psychiatric/medical screenings and behavior state analyses will be part of a comprehensive assessment package that includes functional assessments, which are described in the next chapter.

CHAPTER 6
Functional assessment

Introduction

In assessing challenging behavior there is a need to consider both the context in which the behavior occurs and the function or purpose that the behavior serves. At the level of the individual, when context and function are delineated, one has in a sense explained that person's challenging behavior. This level of understanding and explanation is achieved by undertaking a functional behavioral assessment.

Maag (2000) defined functional assessment as "the process of determining the intent an inappropriate behavior serves for obtaining a desired outcome and replacing that behavior with a more appropriate one that accomplishes the same goal" (p. 136). In more technical terms, a functional assessment is used to identify the variables that control challenging behavior. This includes identifying antecedent variables that set the occasion for challenging behavior as well as identifying the consequences that have shaped and maintained challenging behavior.

Challenging behaviors can be controlled by a variety of antecedents and shaped and maintained by a variety of primary or secondary, positive or negative reinforcers. It is important to note that the challenging behaviors for any given individual can be controlled by numerous antecedents and shaped and maintained by numerous consequences. That is, in many cases challenging behavior can be multiply determined.

In speaking about the reinforcing consequences that shape and maintain challenging behavior, it is helpful to think in terms of function and purpose. Consider an adolescent who has frequent tantrums at school, but only when he is presented with certain task demands. The function or purpose of the tantrum could be to escape from or avoid those task demands. As will be described further later in this chapter, for many individuals with developmental disabilities, the function or purpose of their challenging behaviors is often related to one or more social-communicative functions. These social-communicative functions can be classified as: (a) gaining attention, (b) gaining access to preferred objects or activities, and/or (c) escaping from or avoiding non-preferred objects or activities. In other cases, however, challenging behavior may be shaped and maintained by nonsocial variables, such as sensory stimulation that arises as a direct result of engaging in the behavior. The child may engage in stereotyped movements, for example, because of the "reinforcing perceptual stimuli it produces" (Lovaas, Newsom and Hickman, 1987, p. 45).

Functional assessments can be designed to assist clinicians in discovering why the person engages in challenging behavior. This information would have considerable implications for treatment. That is, it is important to identify the variables controlling challenging behavior. Once these variables are identified, it might be possible to manipulate them to reduce challenging behavior (see Chapter 7). For example, if a student tantrums to escape from difficult academic tasks, a useful intervention may be to initially reduce the difficulty level of the tasks and then gradually reintroduce more difficult tasks using errorless learning procedures (DePaepe, Shores and Jack, 1996). In terms of designing educational interventions to address challenging behavior, it is first important to identify the function or purpose of challenging behavior. Once the function or purpose is identified, educational intervention can focus on teaching the individual more appropriate forms of behavior to achieve that same function or purpose.

A functional assessment is the means by which controlling variables are isolated and the function or purpose of challenging behavior is identified. In terms of treatment, functional assessment methodology has revolutionized the effectiveness of behavioral and educational treatments for challenging behavior as will be reviewed in Chapter 7. Functional assessment data may enable a clinician to develop a hypothesis about the function or purpose of challenging behavior. Intervention plans are then developed based on the hypothesis. As Durand and Crimmins (1991) explained, this functional approach to treatment selection is quite different (and more likely to be both effective and efficient) from an empirical approach where promising treatments are implemented on a trial and error basis. At a conceptual and theoretical level, a functional assessment may provide data leading to a better understanding and explanation of challenging behavior. At a practical level, a functional assessment may provide data that will enable clinicians to develop more effective interventions.

Given its theoretical and applied relevance, it is not surprising that a range of functional assessment procedures have been developed and adapted for use in various settings such as home, school, community and clinic (Larson and Maag, 1998). Functional assessment methodologies have also been used with good results for a variety of disability conditions including autism and related developmental disabilities, ADHD, emotional and behavioral disorders, and specific learning difficulties (Artesani and Mallar, 1998; Heckaman et al., 2000; Reid and Maag, 1998; Scott et al., 2000). It is an approach that has considerable generality.

Regardless of the population with which – or setting in which – this approach is used, the importance of an accompanying intervention program that considers not only function and purpose, but also issues such as quality of life, social validity, and practicality cannot be over-stated (Sugai, Horner and Sprague, 1999). Functional assessment procedures are tools to help clinicians understand and explain challenging behavior and then use this better understanding and explanation to design more effective behavioral and educational treatments. Behavioral and educational treatments are, in turn, enhanced by including a comprehensive array of related services that are focused on improving the person's overall quality of life.

As mentioned earlier, this more comprehensive focus is what is meant by the term positive behavior support or PBS. As explained by Carr et al. (2002), PBS aims to integrate behavioral and educational interventions with more global interventions that involve lifestyle and system changes. PBS is therefore multi-faceted, but functional assessment is a critical component in the development of PBS plans to address challenging behavior in individuals with developmental disabilities.

One area that must be addressed in considering functional assessment is personnel training and development, especially given the evolution from behavior management to PBS (Artesani and Mallar, 1998). Scott and Nelson (1999) have argued that until effective training and continuing professional development in the systematic use of functional assessment are provided, no amount of legislative or research imperatives will achieve the translation of these techniques into typical settings, such as home, school and community. They note that "the key to effective implementation of a functional behavioral assessment and intervention model will depend upon trainers' ability to create a comprehensive and interactive training package, encourage school-wide implementation, and facilitate successful outcomes via ongoing support" (p. 251). An underlying aspect in the provision of such professional development is the amount of importance placed upon teaming and collaboration, at a class, school or district level (Arthur et al. 2002; Chandler, 2000; Chandler et al., 1999; Scott and Nelson, 1999). Chandler et al. (1999), for example, demonstrated that it was possible for teams who had received a program of workshops and in-class support in the use of functional assessment to effect positive and sustained changes in student behavior. Along with an emphasis on prevention and intervention, the training and consultation model incorporated the strategic use of case studies, and perhaps most importantly, an applied rather than theoretical focus on experiences in the classroom (Chandler, 2000).

Along these lines, the development of positive behavior support plans at a class, school and district level was addressed in an Australian professional development program reported by Arthur et al. (2002). This statewide program incorporated a practical case application workshop and the formation of district behavior support teams, which aimed to continue training at a school and individual level.

Achieving sustained and meaningful changes in professional practice is a daunting task, regardless of the urgency, logic or evidence of a need for such change. Staff development and support in the use of functional assessment approaches is a critical, but complex aspect of the broader process of research-based innovation in behavior and educational programming. This programming should aim to increase the number of functional adaptive skills in the behavioral repertoires of individuals with developmental disabilities.

Antecedents and consequences

As mentioned before a functional assessment is used to identify the variables that control challenging behaviors. These variables include the antecedent conditions that set the occasion for the behavior and the reinforcing consequences that maintain the behavior.

Antecedent conditions include environmental and biological factors that might predispose the individual to engage in challenging behavior. Environmental antecedents can be viewed as changes in the environment that increase the probability of challenging behavior. Such factors can be highly idiosyncratic. For example, O'Reilly (1999) demonstrated that the amount of social interaction that occurred prior to an activity was associated with the amount of self-injury observed in a man with severe mental retardation. Specifically, if the man did not interact with people for approximately 1 hour prior to activities, he engaged in higher levels of self-injury during activities. In contrast, if he was engaged in high levels of social interaction prior to these same activities, then self-injury was less likely during these activities. Similarly, the presence of physical conditions such as allergies or sleep disturbance can be associated with higher levels of challenging behavior (Kennedy and Meyer, 1996; O'Reilly, 1995). A functional assessment is useful to the extent that it can clarify the antecedent conditions that are associated with differing probabilities of challenging behavior for any given individual.

Consequences, in the present context, refer to changes in the environment that occur as a result of challenging behavior. When the resulting consequence or consequences function to increase the future probability of challenging behavior, then these are properly defined as reinforcers. Reinforcers are related to motivation. They can be viewed as the motivation for challenging behavior. A functional assessment is therefore effective and useful to the extent that it identifies those consequences that have shaped and maintained challenging behavior.

For individuals with developmental disabilities, functional assessments are usually tailored to clarify whether challenging behavior is maintained by or motivated by one of several types of reinforcers. Challenging behavior may be motivated by the fact that in the past it has enabled the individual to gain access to tangible reinforcers, such as access to reinforcing events (e.g. receipt of food, drinks or toys). Challenging behaviors might also occur because in the past it has been followed by attention from others (e.g. social interactions from peers, parents, teachers, etc.) and we can assume that in many cases and under many conditions, this form of attention is a reinforcer for the individual. In terms of negative reinforcement, challenging behaviors may occur because they have enabled the person to escape from or avoid aversive stimulation. Finally, some challenging behaviors may be maintained by reinforcers that arise as a direct result of engaging in the behavior. This is often referred to as automatic reinforcement and it can take the form of sensory stimulation. Self-injury, for example, might produce pleasant internal sensations or may reduce other painful internal sensations (Cataldo and Harris, 1982).

One should now be able to see how the results of a functional assessment might generate the data necessary to explain challenging behavior. In the science of behavior analysis, when the variables that control a behavior are delineated, the behavior has in fact been explained. Asked why a child engages in self-injury, a clinician may answer by pointing to assessment data demonstrating that the behavior is evoked by difficult tasks and maintained by escape from those tasks. The self-injury can then be explained as escape-motivated. In this way, the child's challenging behavior has been explained.

One should now have a better understanding of how it is that a functional assessment leads to treatment selection. Once the function or purpose of the challenging behavior is known, then intervention strategies are selected to match the function or purpose of the person's challenging behavior, much like a doctor prescribes the right medication depending on the diagnosis. A functional assessment can be viewed as a type of behavioral diagnosis (Bailey and Pyles, 1989). That is, functional assessment data often enable the clinician to diagnose the cause or causes of the challenging behavior or behaviors and then select the right type of treatment for that cause, as well as rule out interventions that would not be appropriate. While we discuss intervention strategies in great depth in the next chapter it is very important to note that functional assessment and intervention selection are inextricably linked.

Consider the use of time-out in the treatment of challenging behavior. Time-out might involve removing a person from an activity/environment for a pre-specified period of time contingent upon challenging behavior. Time-out can be an effective intervention for reducing behaviors maintained by positive secondary reinforcers, such as attention from teachers. It would not, however, be indicated for escape-motivated behavior. This is because time-out allows the person to escape, which would be a negative reinforcer for escape-maintained challenging behavior. Thus, if used under certain conditions that a person may find aversive, a time-out procedure may in fact increase the probability of challenging behavior because it allows the individual to escape from these ongoing events. Alternatively, the same time-out procedure when a person is engaged in preferred activities (e.g. interacting with parents, playing with favorite toys) may reduce challenging behavior.

Haring and Kennedy (1990) examined the effects of time-out on challenging behavior under a task and a leisure condition for an individual with severe developmental disabilities. The effects of another intervention, involving the differential reinforcement of other behavior (DRO) were also examined with this individual, but will not be addressed in this discussion. The task condition involved identifying common items such as money and various foods during teaching trials. The leisure condition involved listening to the radio. The person's challenging behavior consisted of stereotyped mannerisms including body rocking, loud vocalizations and spitting. Time-out under the task condition involved stopping the instruction for 15 seconds contingent on stereotyped responding. Time-out under the leisure condition consisted of removing the leisure items (i.e. turning the radio off for 15 seconds) contingent on stereotyped behavior. Time-out under the task and leisure conditions was structurally identical (i.e. removal of the activity when stereotyped behavior occurred). The results showed that the time-out intervention had a different effect on challenging behavior across the two conditions. Specifically, time-out resulted in increases in stereotypy under the task condition and decreases in stereotypy in the leisure condition.

This study nicely illustrates the fact that the function or purpose of challenging behavior needs to be taken into account prior to selecting and implementing behavioral and educational treatments. For the clinician then, it is important to understand the various types of functional assessments that can be used to identify the function or purpose of challenging behavior.

Types of functional assessment

In conducting a functional assessment, one should aim to collect information in all of the environments and situations where the behavior occurs. Doing so may increase the ecological validity of the resulting assessment data. This may also increase the likelihood that the assessment results will include the range of antecedents and consequences that could be influencing the person's behavior. In terms of conducting a functional assessment, there are two general types. These are (a) indirect assessment methods and (b) direct assessment methods.

Indirect assessment

Indirect methods include the use of interviews and rating scales. These methods are indirect in the sense that they do not require direct observation of the person engaging in challenging behavior. Instead, interviews and rating scales rely on subjective verbal reports by a third party to identify the nature of the challenging behavior and the environmental conditions that are controlling it. Those who are interviewed should be in daily contact with the person and therefore be in a position to describe events they have witnessed in the past and draw conclusions about the causes of the individual's behavior.

There are three general goals of the behavioral interview: (a) description of the behavior(s) (i.e. what is the problem? what does it look like?); (b) identification of those physical and environmental influences that seem to predict the challenging behavior (i.e. when does it occur?); and (c) identification of the maintaining consequences (i.e. what consequent events might be functioning as reinforcers for the challenging behavior?). The interview should therefore include probes that ask specifically about the topography of the behavior, the contexts in which the behavior does and does not occur, and the typical reactions of others in the immediate environment to the challenging behavior.

As an example of an indirect assessment that can be helpful in identifying the influence of global antecedent conditions, Gardner et al. (1986) developed the *Setting Event Checklist*. The checklist contains questions about the person's physical condition, mood and possible precipitating social interactions. It also queries how recently such conditions or interactions occurred. Examples of items from the Setting Event Checklist include: Was the person (a) informed of something unusual or disappointing, (b) excessively tired/lethargic, and (c) under the care of someone new?

In addition to this checklist, there are a number of commercially available interview protocols and rating scales that clinicians can use to identify the potential consequences maintaining challenging behavior. Some of these include the *Motivation Assessment Scale* (MAS) (Durand and Crimmins, 1988), the *Questions About Behavioral Function* (QABF) (Paclawskyj et al., 2000), and a *Behavioral Diagnostic* form developed by Jon Bailey and colleagues (Bailey and Pyles, 1989). The MAS, for example, has 16 questions that may help a clinician decide whether the child's behavior is related to (a) attention, (b) escape, (c) tangible or (d) sensory functions.

Because these questionnaires and rating scales are inexpensive, readily available and relatively quick and easy to complete, it is highly recommended that clinicians use these as the first step in a functional assessment. At a minimum, clinicians should try to get answers to four main questions that need to be asked about the person's challenging behavior:

1. Are there any conditions under which this behavior frequently or always occurs?
2. Are there any conditions under which this behavior rarely or never occurs?
3. What types of events or interactions are typically occurring when the behavior starts?
4. Once the behavior starts, what can be done to get the behavior to stop? For example, will the person stop if they are given attention or left alone?

In using indirect methods it is important to remember that there are many questions that could be asked of the person's behavior that might help one identify its function or purpose. It is most helpful to focus on antecedents and consequences that might evoke and maintain the behavior, respectively.

Information obtained from an indirect assessment may enable the clinician to form an educated guess or hypothesis about the function or purpose of the person's challenging behavior. For example, if a person screams when asked to complete a task, this trend might suggest that the person's behavior is used to escape from and avoid the task. Alternatively, if challenging behavior starts when you shift your attention to another person and stops when the person has your undivided attention, then the function of behavior might be related to gaining attention. Hypotheses based on indirect assessment data should be viewed as tentative, however, because indirect assessments procedures are often of unknown reliability and validity. Initial hypotheses should therefore be verified by implementing additional and more direct assessment procedures.

Direct assessment

Direct functional assessment methods involve systematic observation of the person who engages in challenging behavior and the recording of the occurrence/nonoccurrence of the challenging behavior. There are a number of different types of direct observational protocols. These protocols vary in terms of the type of information gathered, level of training needed by staff to implement the protocol, and the amount of effort needed to conduct such observations.

No matter what observation protocol is used, it is first necessary to clarify exactly what is to be observed. Issues related to the description of challenging behaviors were covered in Chapter 1. For our current discussion, it is important to ensure that the challenging behaviors of concern are defined in observable and measurable terms. Too often when a person is initially referred for assessment their challenging behavior is described in terms of personality characteristics or summary labels such as, "My child is very aggressive," or "He is just being naughty when he hits people." These global terms must be translated into overt observable behaviors before one can begin to conduct observations. This clarification is an important step for several reasons. First, it allows for more reliable observations. Second, it clarifies the precise nature of the behavior to be changed. Third, it allows for ongoing evaluation of the challenging behavior throughout the intervention process. If desired change is not occurring then intervention can be altered. We will discuss the importance of providing for the ongoing evaluation of interventions in the next chapter.

To extend the discussion on description of challenging behavior that was begun in Chapter 1, we turn to work by Hawkins and Dobes (1975) who provided three guidelines for developing a clear description of challenging behavior:

1. The description should be objective referring only to observable characteristics of the behavior (and environment) and translating any inferential terms into more objective ones.
2. The description should be clear and unambiguous so that others could read the description and observe the behavior accurately.
3. The description should be complete, delineating the boundaries of what is to be included as an instance of challenging behavior and what is to be excluded. There should be little left to personal judgment.

An example of a clear description of challenging behavior arising from the statement "My child is very aggressive" might be, "Striking siblings in a forceful manner with an open hand or closed fist, but excluding touching siblings with tips of fingers or with an open hand in a nonforceful manner." This description identifies the challenging behaviors in objective terms and delineates examples of behavior to be included and excluded. Consider the following descriptions adapted from Iwata et al. (1994, p. 219), which provide clear descriptions of challenging behaviors:

- Head banging: Audible or forceful contact of the head against a stationary object.
- Biting: Closure of upper and lower teeth on any part of the body.
- Scratching: Raking the skin with fingernails or rubbing against objects.
- Pinching: Forceful grasping of skin between fingers.
- Hair pulling: Closure of fingers on hair with a pulling motion.

Once there is agreement on what to observe, the next step is to choose an observation tool. There are several popular observation tools and a number of ways of conducting such observations. For example, one can observe the behavior of the person during their regular daily routines using such methods as a *Scatterplot* or an *Antecedent–Behavior–Consequence* (A–B–C) method. Alternatively or additionally one can conduct an assessment of challenging behavior by systematically structuring the environment and measuring concomitant changes in behavior.

Scatterplot assessment

The Scatterplot assessment method is probably the easiest direct observation method to use (Touchette, MacDonald and Langer, 1985). This method of assessment provides information about the temporal distribution of behavior (i.e. when during the day the behavior occurs). The Scatterplot method is not designed to identify the antecedents that evoke nor the consequences that motivate challenging behavior. It should therefore be used in conjunction with indirect assessment methods to help clarify the reasons why someone engages in challenging behavior. It can also be used as a preliminary assessment tool to identify periods of time when behavior occurs, which may allow for a more detailed assessment of challenging behavior during those high-frequency time periods.

The first step in conducting a Scatterplot is to design a grid with equal time segments on the vertical axis and days on the horizontal axis. The time segments should suit the particular situation (e.g. 15 min, 30 min, 1 hour). An example of a Scatterplot grid is given in Figure 6.1. You can see that the day (from 9 a.m. to 2:30 p.m.) is broken into cells with each cell representing 30 minutes of the person's day. Next a decision about how to record challenging behavior during each of these 30 minute time periods needs to be made. A Scatterplot does not require the observer to record the exact frequency of occurrence of challenging behavior during each 30-minute period (i.e. there is no need to record every instance of the behavior). Instead, a more general recording procedure can be used.

In Figure 6.1 we used a light gray shading in the cell if there was one occurrence of the challenging behavior during that 30-minute period, we used darker shading in the cell if there were two occurrences, and we filled in the square with black shading if there were three or more occurrences during a 30-minute period.

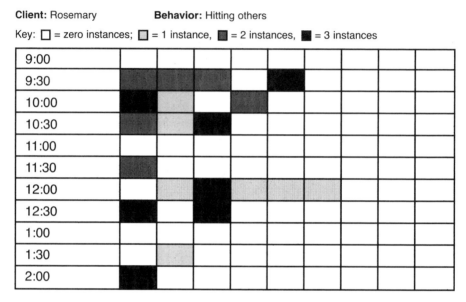

Client: Rosemary   **Behavior:** Hitting others

Key: ☐ = zero instances; ▨ = 1 instance, ▦ = 2 instances, ■ = 3 instances

Figure 6.1 Example of a Scatterplot grid covering five days of observations.

The Scatterplot depicted in Figure 6.1 was used by day-care staff to identify the temporal distribution of "hitting other clients" by a woman with severe intellectual disabilities in a day-care center. The Scatterplot was conducted over six days. You will notice that challenging behavior occurs most frequently between 9:30 a.m. and 10:30 a.m. and between 11:30 a.m. and 12:30 p.m. These times correspond to when the young woman was engaged in vocational training. Further assessment is now needed to clarify the reasons for why she might be engaging in this challenging behavior during vocational training. It is also interesting to note that her challenging behavior is more severe on Days 1 and 3 of the assessment. Interviews with staff indicated that this young woman had less than five hours' sleep the nights prior to Days 1 and 3 of the assessment. This implies that poor sleep patterns may be influencing the severity of this person's challenging behavior.

Antecedent–behavior–consequence (A–B–C)

To use this method, the clinician needs to be able to set aside time to observe the person over at least 3–4 days. During these times, the clinician watches the person and when challenging behavior occurs, a brief description of what the person did is recorded. The description includes the behavior plus the antecedents and consequences that related to that behavior. An example of an ABC recording is shown in Table 6.1.

Table 6.1 A–B–C recording sheet and example

Child: Sheri   **Date & time of observation:** April 15, 10:15 –10:45

Instance number	What was happening at the time?	What did the child do that was a problem?	What happened in response to the child's behavior?
1	The tantrum started when the teacher pulled out a pen and paper and tried to get Sheri to copy letters.	She started screaming and dropped to the floor. Once on the floor she kept screaming and started to bang her head on the floor.	The teacher told Sheri to stand up. Sheri kept screaming and lying on the floor. After 1 minute of trying to talk Sheri into standing up, the teacher gave up and left the area. Sheri gradually calmed down. She stopped screaming and stopped banging her head. She moved to a corner of the room by herself.
2	The class was returning from the playground to the classroom.	She screamed and fell to the floor when we got close to the door.	She was allowed to play outside for a few more minutes and then the clinician coaxed her into the room by offering her a treat.
3	Lunchtime had just finished and she was told to go back to class.	She screamed and fell to the floor from her chair.	She was left where she was for about a minute and then the clinician offered her a sip of juice to sit down.

After recording what the person did in each instance, the observer describes what was happening when the behavior started. This information goes in the second column of the table. The final column is used to record what people did in response to the person's behavior. The second column is meant to identify possible antecedents to the behavior, whereas the final column is meant to identify possible consequences that might be maintaining the behavior. Three instances are included in Table 6.1. These instances will give you an idea of the level of detail that should be recorded when using an A–B–C analysis. It should be clear from this example that an A–B–C assessment requires significant effort on the part of the observer. For example, it would be difficult for a teacher or parent to continue with routine activities while conducting such an assessment. However, the A–B–C could be targeted for specific times of the day where behavior has been identified as most problematic (through a prior Scatterplot assessment). Identifying circumscribed time periods within which to conduct the A–B–C may make it a more practical approach for clinical practice.

Our experience suggests that at least 20 instances of challenging behavior need to be recorded before trying to interpret the results from an A–B–C analysis. Once you have described 20 or more instances in this manner, it may be possible to see a pattern to the behavior. Remember at this stage, you are looking for evidence as to the function of the behavior.

Although an A–B–C can be a useful supplement to indirect assessment methods, it is often difficult to interpret the data from an A–B–C analysis. The data for Sheri, for example, suggest that she might have been using her challenging behaviors to get out of doing things that she does not want to do, such as escaping from academic activities. She might also have learned that she can get things that she wants (i.e. to be left alone or receive a snack or drink) if she has tantrums.

When the results of a Scatterplot or an A–B–C analysis are consistent with the results of an indirect assessment, then the clinician would have greater confidence in the accuracy of the initial educated guess about the function or purpose of the person's challenging behavior. On the other hand, it is sometimes difficult to interpret the results of these assessments. Such problems can occur when the person's behavior serves multiple functions such as being attention-motivated and escape-motivated or when some unknown variable is influencing the person's behavior. In these cases, a more intensive functional assessment that involves exposing the person to different conditions to see what effect these have on the frequency of challenging behavior is indicated. In most cases, however, at least some of the variables influencing the person's challenging behavior will become evident following the initial screening and review of functional assessment results. Once some of these variables have been identified, appropriate interventions can be selected and implemented.

Functional analysis

The final direct assessment that we will describe is the experimental-functional analysis methodology pioneered by Brian Iwata and his colleagues (Iwata et al., 1982; 1994). An experimental-functional analysis involves a systematic examination of the person's challenging behavior under a number of predetermined social conditions. These social conditions are constructed in such a manner to identify the specific consequences that are maintaining challenging behavior. Generally a functional analysis consists of exposing the person to at least four social conditions (see below). The specific contents of these conditions will be determined on an individual basis based on prior interviews and observations (i.e. if access to specific toys or escape from specific tasks seem to maintain challenging behavior then these will be included in the functional analysis).

The initial report on this procedure (Iwata et al., 1982; 1994) described an assessment conducted in an inpatient unit at the Kennedy Center of Johns Hopkins University School of Medicine. The authors were working with nine children with severe intellectual disability who were referred to this inpatient unit due to chronic self-injury. Each child was systematically and repeatedly exposed (with each session lasting 15 minutes) to four social conditions. The child's challenging behavior was continuously measured during all sessions. Sessions were terminated if self-injury became severe. These four social conditions are described below.

Social attention
In the attention condition the child was placed in a room with a therapist. The therapist directed the child to play with toys that were available in the room. The therapist ignored the child (proceeded to do some paperwork at a table). If the child began to engage in self-injury the therapist immediately attended to the child with statements such as, "Don't hit yourself" while giving the child brief and gentle physical contact (e.g. placing hand on shoulder). The therapist then went back to work and ignored the child until the child again engaged in self-injury. This condition was designed to assess whether self-injury was maintained by attention from others (i.e. positively reinforced by attention). Again several 15-minute sessions of this condition were conducted during the functional analysis.

Academic demand
During the demand condition the therapist worked with the child on educational tasks that the child had difficulty completing. The therapist used a three-step instructional protocol (verbal prompt, model plus verbal prompt, and physical guidance) to complete the task. If the child engaged in self-injury the therapist removed the task and turned away from the child for 30 seconds. The task was removed in this manner when the child engaged in self-injury throughout each 15-minute session. This condition was designed to assess whether self-injury was maintained by escape from tasks (i.e. negatively reinforced by escape).

Alone
The child was placed in a therapy room on their own without access to toys or other materials that might act as sources of external stimulation.

This condition was designed to assess whether self-injury was maintained by internal sources of stimulation (i.e. automatically reinforced). If some forms of self-injury are maintained by consequences of a sensory nature then we would expect to see higher levels of self-injury in situations where there is little external stimulation.

Play
In the play condition the therapist maintained close contact with the child and allowed the child to engage in isolate play or cooperative play. The therapist praised the child and gave brief physical contact for no self-injury approximately every 30 seconds. Self-injury was ignored by the therapist during sessions. This condition served as a control for the other conditions in that a therapist and materials were present, attention was delivered for appropriate behavior and withheld for self-injury, and no demands were presented.

The results from these functional-experimental analyses showed that self-injury varied within and between individuals. For some children, self-injury occurred most frequently in the academic demand condition, suggesting that the behavior was maintained by escape from aversive tasks. In other cases, self-injury did not seem to be sensitive to changes in social conditions, suggesting that the behavior was maintained by some form of sensory consequences (automatic reinforcement). Control by automatic reinforcement is implicated when challenging behavior occurs primarily and most frequently in the alone condition. In still other cases, self-injury seemed to be maintained by multiple consequences in that high rates of self-injury might be observed in both the academic demand and the social attention conditions, for example. Such results would imply that the child has learned to use their self-injury as a means to access attention and to escape from aversive situations.

Results from functional analyses indicate that the exact same behavior (e.g. self-injury) can serve different functions for different individuals. Such findings bolster our earlier emphasis on the importance of conducting assessments to identify factors maintaining challenging behavior on a case-by-case basis. This allows the clinician to tailor interventions to the needs of that individual. Conducting such functional analyses does however take a considerable amount of time, effort and training. Such assessments may not be practical in many applied settings (e.g. a classroom). However, this does not mean that students could not be referred to a specialist therapeutic setting for such assessments when warranted. Functional analysis methods, while originally developed to assess self-injury have been successfully adapted to assess the function of other challenging behaviors, such as aggression, property destruction and feeding disorders with this population.

In conducting an experimental-functional analysis, one must be aware of one of the fundamental principles in the theory of challenging behavior that was delineated in Chapter 3. That fundamental principle is that all human behavior is shaped by its consequences. In an experimental-functional analysis, the behavior occurs and is followed by specific types of consequences. This is done in an effort to determine if the challenging behavior is sensitive to one or more of these various consequences. The intent is to identify the consequences that have already affected and influenced the challenging behavior. The assumption is that whatever consequence the behavior is sensitive to must have already been established as a reinforcer for the behavior prior to the experimental-functional assessment.

However, one should not rule out the possibility that in some cases by exposing the person to the contingencies of an experimental-functional analysis, one might be shaping the challenging behavior. Shaping could occur and might affect both the topography and probability of challenging behavior. This does not mean that an experimental-functional analysis is not useful, but it does mean that clinicians using such procedures must be aware that such procedures could inadvertently shape the challenging behavior in unintended directions. This is why considerable expertise is required to complete experimental-functional analyses of challenging behavior.

Summary and conclusion

After screening for medical conditions that might influence challenging behavior and either ruling out such factors or treating any identified medical conditions (Chapter 5), the next step in developing a successful intervention for challenging behavior is to conduct a functional assessment of that behavior. Functional assessment includes various protocols, but the intent of each is to identify the environmental variables that set the occasion for and maintain challenging behavior. Functional assessments can be integrated with medical screening to identify complex interactions between environmental and medical/biological variables. For example, a person may be more prone to aggression when presented with task demands, but only when they are ill; not when healthy.

Functional assessments explain challenging behavior at the individual level in the sense of identifying its controlling variables. For example, if tantrums can be shown to occur when attention is diverted from the person because the consequence is that others then give the person attention, the challenging behavior is properly understood and explained as attention-motivated.

Functional assessments can be indirect or direct. Indirect assessments involve interviews with or questionnaires completed by third party informants. A good informant is one who interacts with the person regularly. Direct assessments involve systematic observation of the person who engages in challenging behavior. We described three direct observation methods: Scatterplot, A–B–C analysis, and the experimental-functional analysis methodology. These direct methods differ with respect to the type of information they provide, the amount of effort needed to implement each method, and the level of training needed to accurately conduct and interpret each method. It is recommended that at least one indirect and one direct method be used with any individual case. Extreme care is required and a high level of expertise necessary to conduct experimental-functional analysis of challenging behaviors. The latter is a powerful assessment tool, but it may also shape the very behavior that it is intended to assess. This stems from the fact that challenging behavior might be influenced by the prevailing contingencies of reinforcement. An experimental-functional analysis exposes the person to several types of contingencies involving specific and potentially reinforcing consequences and it does so repeatedly and on a consistent basis, which may shape new forms and new operant functions for existing challenging behaviors.

PART 4

TREATMENT AND PREVENTION

CHAPTER 7

Educational and behavioral interventions

Introduction

While some instances of challenging behavior might be effectively managed without the need for systematic assessment and intervention, effective support will often require a formal and comprehensive approach to assessment and intervention. This argument is based on evidence showing that challenging behaviors are unlikely to resolve with the mere passage of time and in the absence of a well-designed intervention (Tonge and Einfeld, 1991). In fact, challenging behaviors left untreated tend to get worse (Einfeld and Tonge, 1996).

Intervention is necessary to prevent the negative consequences of challenging behavior. These negative consequences can include injury to the individual with developmental disabilities and to others, damage to property, disruption to the learning environment, and rejection by peers. People with developmental disabilities and challenging behaviors are more likely to be placed in restrictive residential, educational and vocational settings. This means that in many cases the individual will be denied the benefits of family life and the opportunity to interact with typical peers. Persons with developmental disabilities and challenging behaviors are also frequently prescribed medications to control challenging behaviors, which are not necessarily effective in selectively reducing challenging behaviors. These medications can also have serious health side-effects (see Chapter 5).

Thus a comprehensive intervention plan is required when there is a consistent pattern of challenging behavior. Details of the intervention are contained in a Positive Behavior Support Plan (PBSP). An interdisciplinary team of people that includes the parents and professionals (such as psychologists, special educators and speech pathologists) develops the PBSP. Once developed, members of the team must be trained to implement the plan. In addition, an ongoing evaluation component must be built into the plan so that implementation can be monitored to ensure consistency and to make sure the intervention is having the desired effect.

While some challenging behaviors might be managed informally, an inappropriate response by the clinician may mean that some challenging behaviors can develop and worsen over time. It is therefore important for clinicians to understand the factors that contribute to challenging behaviors as discussed in Chapters 2 and 6, so that they can take steps to prevent the occasional inappropriate behavior from becoming a frequent and severe behavioral challenge. Even if a clinician is not implementing a formal behavioral program, it is important to be aware that the contingencies operating in the environment are always influencing the person's challenging behaviors and that the person's challenging behaviors are, in turn, always influencing the clinician.

The focus of this chapter is on behavioral and educational interventions, but practitioners must also realize that some individuals with developmental disabilities may require other types of interventions because of the nature of their challenging behavior. For example, some individuals may require input from medical or mental health specialists. A clinician must therefore know when to seek referral for outside specialist help and this will necessitate a thorough medical and psychiatric screening as discussed in Chapter 5.

A range of behavioral and educational interventions can be used to reduce challenging behavior in people with developmental disabilities. The important issue in selecting which of the many available options to use is to make sure that the strategy matches the function of the challenging behavior, which is determined by a prior functional assessment as explained in Chapter 6. There are strategies that make sense when the behavior is attention-motivated, but not when the behavior is escape-motivated and vice versa. The aim of this chapter is to describe general strategic approaches to modify attention-motivated, tangible-motivated, escape-motivated, and sensory-motivated challenging behaviors, given that functional assessment data indicate that a majority of challenging behaviors in persons with developmental disabilities can be classified into one or more of these operant-function categories (Iwata et al., 1994). The intent is not to provide a menu of options, but rather to describe classes or types of strategies. It is important to individualize intervention and this means matching the intervention strategies to the function or purpose of the behavior.

We noted in Chapter 6 that it is important to take into account those experiences or conditions that may predispose a person to engage in challenging behavior (antecedent conditions) and those outcomes or changes in the person's environment (consequences) that maintain challenging behavior. These antecedents and consequences can be idiosyncratic and thus need to be identified on a case-by-case basis. Likewise, interventions will often need to be idiosyncratic and tailored to antecedent and consequent conditions that set the occasion for and maintain challenging behavior for that particular person.

In the remainder of this chapter we will discuss some general strategies that have been effective in treating challenging behavior. These strategies are not a panacea, but evidence shows that they can be helpful for designing interventions when matched to the results of a functional assessment. The general strategic approach includes (a) ongoing monitoring of challenging behavior, (b) antecedent interventions, and (c) interventions based on the function of challenging behavior. In the latter category, intervention approaches will be delineated for attention-motivated, tangibly-motivated, escape-motivated and sensory-motivated challenging behavior.

Ongoing monitoring of challenging behavior

The assessment process does not end once a functional assessment has been completed. Instead, a functional assessment should be seen as the first part of the assessment process. Another equally important assessment component involves the ongoing monitoring of challenging behavior. To clarify, one important aspect of an intervention is to evaluate whether or not the intervention actually works. Does the intervention produce a reduction in challenging behavior? One might argue that an effective intervention should be self-evident. That is, when the intervention is implemented the challenging behavior is eliminated. However, interventions may not produce immediate changes in challenging behavior, the reductions in challenging behavior may be gradual, or the intervention may not have the desired effect in terms of reducing challenging behavior. It is best to avoid impressions about changes in challenging behavior and to ground the evaluation of the intervention with some form of measurement of change (or lack thereof) in challenging behavior. Another advantage of ongoing monitoring is that it provides all those who have an interest in the intervention (e.g. other professionals who may have devised the intervention, but who are not responsible for its implementation) with an objective evaluation of the effects of the intervention.

The person with primary responsibility for implementing the intervention will also be the person who conducts the ongoing evaluation of challenging behavior. Ongoing monitoring should therefore be a simple process. For example, parents or teachers, who are frequently the primary interventionists, have many responsibilities that can make ongoing assessment a difficult task to accomplish. We present a simple method of ongoing monitoring in the remainder of this section.

One of the first essential components of ongoing monitoring is accomplished as part of the functional assessment. That is, we first need a clear definition and description of the challenging behavior as discussed in Chapters 1 and 6. Next the therapist should assess the level or frequency of challenging behavior prior to the intervention. This gives a clear impression of what the behavior is like immediately prior to the intervention and allows for a pre–post comparison. We suggest that the clinician conduct such an assessment for anywhere between 3 and 7 days before the intervention. Technically, the aim is to obtain a stable baseline of the challenging behavior before starting the intervention and then to measure challenging behavior throughout the entire day during this period. We also suggest a simple measurement system, such as a frequency count. For example, a parent could keep a piece of paper with a description of the challenging behavior in an immediate yet safe place. When the behavior occurs the parent could place a check mark on the sheet to indicate an occurrence. At the end of the day, the number of occurrences could be tallied and the total frequency of challenging behavior for that day could be inserted on a graph.

Antecedent interventions

We have previously emphasized the importance of identifying antecedent conditions that may influence challenging behavior. In Chapter 6, we described interview strategies that might be used as part of a functional assessment to identify potential antecedent influences. Antecedent conditions do not cause challenging behavior per se, but rather they set the occasion for challenging behavior. It was not until recent years that antecedent conditions received attention from clinicians. Up until recently interventions were almost solely based on manipulating consequences contingent upon challenging behavior. Identifying and changing consequences for challenging behavior are still very important from an assessment and intervention perspective (as we will see later in this chapter). In fact many comprehensive interventions will involve modification of antecedent conditions and the manipulation of consequences to treat challenging behavior.

Antecedent influences can be distilled into two broad categories – each with distinct clinical implications. Social/ecological conditions include environmental conditions (e.g. a cold classroom, a cramped environment, sparse environmental or low stimulation conditions) or interactions with individuals (e.g. a disliked staff person, being bullied). These conditions or interactions may increase the likelihood of challenging behavior. From a clinical point of view, it may be possible to identify and remove such conditions. For example, a person could be moved to a more pleasant living or working environment, the current environment could be made more stimulating, and interactions between the person with challenging behavior and contact with a disliked staff member could be minimized. In other words, challenging behavior can be made less probable when a social/ecological condition is removed or remedied.

For example, Kennedy and Itkonen (1993) worked with a student with profound disabilities who engaged in aggression towards others (hitting) and self-injury (pulling her own hair). The authors noted that on some days her behavior was quite severe during school while on other days it was quite low. Initially, the authors assessed the number of times she engaged in challenging behaviors across the entire school day. This initial assessment was the baseline. They found that on the first day of baseline, the student engaged in 20 episodes of challenging behavior while on the second and third days of baseline she engaged in two and four episodes of challenging behavior, respectively. On the fourth day of baseline, she engaged in 15 episodes of challenging behavior. They also noted that challenging behavior was more severe during the first and fourth days when it took her longer to get to school because of the bus route. The intervention consisted of a travel program, whereby she was driven to school on her usual and less time-consuming route. Challenging behavior was a lot less severe during school days when the travel program was in place. Here we have an example of a routine (a particular route to school) that when disturbed was associated with high levels of challenging behavior during the day. The antecedent intervention, which ensured that the less time-consuming routine was followed, resulted in lower levels of challenging behavior.

In some circumstances, even when an antecedent ecological or social condition is identified, it may not be possible to modify such conditions. For example, a student may not like a particular teacher, but it may not be possible to change the teacher. In these situations it may be necessary to focus on alternative strategies, such as teaching communication skills and enriching the current environment to manage challenging behavior.

The other broad category of antecedent variables that may predispose persons to engage in challenging behavior are termed bio-behavioral conditions. Bio-behavioral conditions can be subdivided into conditions that can be of a permanent or temporary influence. An example of a permanent biological condition might be medical or behavioral predispositions that accompany various genetic syndromes. Certain genetic syndromes such as Down's syndrome or Williams syndrome are associated with developmental disability. Some of these syndromes have accompanying biological or behavioral traits. For example, individuals with Cornelia de Lange syndrome suffer from intestinal difficulties that may cause these individuals to be in pain. Many individuals with Cornelia de Lange syndrome engage in self-injury to the torso (i.e. skin picking and tearing around the chest and stomach). The primary intervention, or at least the initial evaluations, should be medical in nature (i.e. to identify possible discomfort and to reduce the physical discomfort). For individuals with Williams syndrome many ordinary noises such as those from a vacuum cleaner or lawnmower may be intolerable (a condition known as hyperacusis). This condition can in turn produce aggressive behavior. O'Reilly, Lacey and Lancioni (2000) demonstrated a relationship between overall noise level and aggressive outbursts for a child with Williams syndrome in a regular classroom. O'Reilly et al. equipped this child with earplugs during noisy classroom situations and this reduced aggression. Another example is from children with autism who may display repetitive behaviors that if interfered with can cause aggression and self-injury (Murphy et al., 2000).

From a clinical perspective it may be important to identify the presence of genetic syndromes or conditions and to be aware of possible predispositions caused by such conditions in terms of potential triggers for challenging behavior. The impact of such genetic predispositions can be minimized by altering environmental arrangements or by direct medical monitoring and intervention.

Other biological conditions can be temporary in nature. Conditions such as illness, allergies, ear infections or sleep disturbance may increase the likelihood of challenging behavior. These conditions should be identified and treated with such individuals. For example, O'Reilly (1997) examined head hitting for a young child with developmental disability over an extended period of time. The child engaged in high levels of head hitting on some occasions, but not on others. Medical examinations indicated that the child only engaged in head hitting when she was also diagnosed with ear infections. It can be inferred that she hit her head to reduce the discomfort associated with the ear infection.

Pyles and Bailey (1992) demonstrated the influence of menstruation on head banging and head hitting for a woman with profound disabilities. High levels of head banging occurred during menstruation prior to intervention. Little head banging occurred outside of menstruation. During intervention, Motrin was prescribed for pain relief. This produced dramatic reductions in head banging during menstruation. These results indicate that it is important to account for transient biological conditions such as illness or allergies as they may contribute to challenging behavior. Such biological conditions should be treated as part of the intervention program.

Interventions based on consequence manipulation

We have discussed the importance of identifying antecedent conditions and selecting interventions to reduce the impact of such conditions on challenging behavior in the last section. In Chapter 6, we emphasized the importance of identifying consequences that maintain challenging behavior. We noted in Chapter 6 that challenging behavior with this population can be influenced by such consequences as attention from others, access to favorite items, escape from aversive tasks, or automatic consequences. Once we have identified potential consequences that seem to influence the probability of challenging behavior, we need to develop interventions based on this information. The aim of this section is to describe strategies that would be used to modify attention-motivated, tangible-motivated, escape-motivated and sensory-motivated challenging behaviors. The intent is not to provide a menu of options, but rather to describe a package of strategies that would be indicated for each of these four distinct functions.

Arranging positive consequences for appropriate behavior and eliminating positive consequences for challenging behavior is an important part of any intervention. In addition, other types of corrective consequences may also be necessary. Negative feedback can help a person to learn what is right and what is wrong. In selecting consequences, it is important to consider the use of natural consequences that provide feedback without special intervention. For example, when a child rips up his coloring book, the natural consequence is that he no longer has a coloring book to use. Similarly, when a child spills her juice on the floor the natural consequence is that she no longer has any juice to drink.

Another important issue in behavioral and educational treatments is related to the selection of consequences. Regardless of what else occurs, it is fundamental to arrange contingencies so that appropriate behavior is reinforced and challenging behavior is not. Punishing consequences may also be necessary to reduce challenging behaviors in some cases, and it may be justifiable to use aversive procedures when less intrusive efforts have not been effective (see Chapter 4).

Intervention for attention-motivated challenging behavior

As we explained in Chapter 6, some challenging behaviors appear to be learned as a way of getting attention. That is, the maintaining consequence is attention from others. Challenging behaviors may emerge as a means of gaining attention if the repertoire contains few, if any, alternative responses that are effective in recruiting attention. In these situations, attention is a reinforcer. We need not ask why it is a reinforcer, but one could do so and by doing so one might discover that for several reasons attention is very important to the individual. That is, if the person starts hitting or kicking to gain the attention of others, then this would suggest that the attention is a powerful reinforcer.

Armed with this knowledge, the clinician can therefore use attention in ways that will reinforce appropriate behavior and reduce challenging behavior. There are four main strategies for reducing attention-motivated challenging behavior. In many cases it will be appropriate and more effective to use all four strategies at the same time.

Increase the overall level of attention

When attention is the maintaining consequence for challenging behavior, one way to decrease challenging behavior is to increase the overall amount of attention that the person receives. For example, the clinician might set a kitchen timer for varying intervals of time (e.g. three minutes, one minute, five minutes, two minutes) and when the timer goes off, the individual receives 10–20 seconds of positive attention. Technically, this procedure is known as noncontingent reinforcement because the reinforcement (attention) is delivered on a fixed-time schedule irrespective of the child's behavior (Tucker, Sigafoos and Bushell, 1998). As the individual starts to receive more attention than usual under this fixed-time schedule, there is likely to be less need for that person to engage in attention-motivated challenging behavior.

Provide attention for appropriate behavior

A variation on the use of noncontingent attention is to provide positive attention to the individual for the absence of challenging behavior. The idea is to catch the individual when they are not engaging in challenging behavior and deliver reinforcement at these times. As the person learns that attention is received without having to resort to challenging behavior, then challenging behavior should become less likely. A potential side benefit is that appropriate behavior may increase. Technically, this procedure is known as differential reinforcement of other behavior. As with noncontingent reinforcement, the reinforcer takes the form of positive attention from the practitioner. This could be a kind word, a hug, a smile, as well as spending some time conversing with the person about something that interests him or her. The important point is to provide attention for the absence of challenging behavior.

A variation is to provide attention, not just for the absence of challenging behavior but also for the presence of appropriate alternative behavior.

Extinction

Along with attention for appropriate behavior, the clinician should ignore challenging behaviors as much as possible. If the behavior must be attended to, then it should be done as matter of factly as possible. Even negative attention in the form of a reprimand may be a reinforcer for attention-motivated challenging behavior. If challenging behavior occurs because the person has learned to use it to gain attention, then the clinician must turn the situation around and teach the person that challenging behavior will no longer work as a way of getting attention, but rather attention will be given only for appropriate behavior.

Teach attention gaining skills

In some cases the individual may resort to challenging behaviors to gain attention because they lack more appropriate ways of gaining attention. The repertoire is limited and available options are less efficient than challenging behavior. In such cases, a useful strategy might be to teach the individual a better way of gaining attention. For example, the person might be taught to seek attention ('Will you sit with me?') so that others will come over and spend some time with the person. When teaching alternative attention gaining behaviors the important point is to prompt the new behavior before the person begins to engage in challenging behavior.

Intervention for tangible-motivated challenging behavior

The basic principles and strategies for tangible-motivated challenging behaviors are similar to those for attention-motivated challenging behavior. Some challenging behaviors appear to be learned as a way of getting access to preferred objects and activities. In these situations, the clinician should realize that access to these items and activities is a reinforcer of importance to the individual. That is, if a person becomes aggressive or has a tantrum in order to gain access to some preferred object, then this would suggest the object is highly valued at least at that particular moment. The clinician should therefore be able to use access to the preferred object in ways that will reinforce appropriate behavior and reduce challenging behavior. There are four main strategies that can be used to reduce tangible-motivated challenging behavior. In many cases it will be appropriate and more effective to use all four strategies at the same time.

Increase the overall level of access

When gaining access to a preferred object or activity maintains challenging behavior, then, one way to decrease the behavior is to increase the overall amount of access to preferred objects and activities. For example, access to preferred items or activities could be scheduled on some regular basis (e.g. 20 minutes). This technique is similar to the use of noncontingent reinforcement for attention-motivated challenging behavior.

Provide access for appropriate behavior

Another strategy is to provide access to preferred objects and activities as reinforcement for the absence of challenging behavior. The idea is to teach the individual that challenging behavior is not necessary and that reinforcement will occur without the need to resort to challenging behavior. As the individual starts to receive access to preferred objects and activities for appropriate behavior, he or she will be more likely to engage in appropriate behavior and hence there will be less time for challenging behavior. This is similar to the use of differential reinforcement of other behavior or differential reinforcement of alternative behavior. The reinforcer in this case takes the form of access to some preferred object or activity for a period of time. The important point is to provide the highly valued object or activity for the absence of challenging behavior and contingent upon some more appropriate alternative behavior.

Extinction

Along with giving access to preferred objects or activities for appropriate behavior, the intervention plan should specify that challenging behaviors will no longer enable the individual to gain access to preferred objects and activities. Tangible-motivated challenging behavior persists because the behavior has been reinforced by at least occasional access to preferred objects and activities. The extinction procedure is used to turn the situation around and teach the person that challenging behavior will not result in access to preferred objects or activities.

Teach appropriate requesting skills

In some cases the individual may resort to challenging behaviors to get things that he or she wants or needs because more appropriate ways of requesting those items are not in the person's repertoire. In such cases, a useful strategy involves teaching the person a better way of requesting access to preferred objects or activities. When teaching alternative requesting behaviors, the important point is to prompt the new behavior before challenging behavior has a chance to occur. In addition to teaching requesting, it may be useful to teach the person how to get access to preferred items or activities independently. Again this involves building new behaviors.

Intervention for escape-motivated challenging behavior

A number of strategies exist for reducing escape-motivated challenging behaviors. Clinicians may find that one or more of the strategies will be relevant to the management of challenging behaviors.

Reinforce participation

If challenging behavior is reinforced by escape from non-preferred activities, then the intervention plan should include reinforcement contingent upon increasing levels of participation. Initially, for example, an adolescent in a vocational training program might be prompted to complete one piece of work and then receive reinforcement. Potential reinforcers might include praise (e.g. "Good job!"), access to a preferred object, and being allowed to take a break from the task. Over time, the adolescent is required to participate for longer periods of time before receiving reinforcement. In this way the clinician can increase participation and reduce challenging behaviors that were previously used to escape from the vocational task.

Escape extinction

Another strategy is to make sure that challenging behaviors are no longer effective in procuring negative reinforcement in the form of escape and avoidance. That is the intervention plan should specify that attempts to escape from the task involving challenging behavior would no longer enable the person to escape from or avoid the task. To use this procedure effectively means that the clinician must be prepared to persist with instruction even if the challenging behavior escalates. In addition to extinction, when appropriate participation occurs, reinforcement is provided.

Reduce task difficulty

In some cases challenging behavior may occur during task demands because the task is too difficult. In such cases, the clinician should try to make the task easier and use errorless learning procedures to gradually increase the difficulty level. In other cases, the clinician might teach the individual to ask for help with difficult tasks.

Task preference

In other cases, challenging behavior may occur because the task is less preferred than some other available activity. In such cases, the clinician might simply decide to eliminate the less preferred task from the routine (if possible), introduce reinforcement for participation, and/or give the individual a choice of what activities to engage in and when. For example, the individual might be given a choice as to whether to do a task now or later.

Task duration

Sometimes a person will participate in a task for a period of time and then engage in challenging behavior to make it known that he or she has had enough. In these cases, intervention consists of providing more frequent breaks and gradually increasing the length of the task.

Transition issues

Some individuals seem to have difficulty moving from one activity to another. Their difficulty may be expressed as challenging behavior when they are required to stop one activity and begin some other activity. These behaviors could be interpreted as avoidance in the sense that the individual may be attempting to avoid the transition. Several strategies can be used in such situations. First, it may help to introduce a picture schedule and use this to cue the individual as to when one activity ends and what is next. The person can receive reinforcement for following the picture schedule. Picture schedules can help in cases where the person may not fully comprehend the verbal instructions that are provided. Another way to deal with transition problems is to offer the person a choice from among the options on the picture schedule. If the schedule includes four activities that must be completed over the day, the clinician can allow the person to choose which one to do first, second, third and fourth, for example.

Interventions for sensory-motivated challenging behavior

When challenging behavior is maintained by sensory consequences (automatic reinforcement), the clinician should look for ways to enrich the environment, as was done by Horner in his classic 1980 study (see Chapter 4). The idea is to provide more meaningful activities in the environment so that the person will have less need to seek stimulation through challenging behavior. An important component of this strategy is to find more appropriate activities that are also preferred by the individual. Once identified, the person may need to be taught how to participate in those activities.

Environmental enrichment

The environment can be enriched in a number of general ways. First, it is important to identify items and activities that are preferred by the person. This can be done by talking to parents or staff who interact regularly with the person. It may also be worthwhile to incorporate activities/items that are known to be preferred by the person based on past history. One can also conduct a more systematic preference assessment by exposing the person to items/activities on several occasions. When the person is exposed to these items/activities you should note how they react. Do they smile when the item is presented? Do they reach for the item? Do they frown and push the item away? If the person seems to regularly enjoy the item/activity when it is presented then this could be incorporated into the person's daily activities. If the person does not seem to like the item/activity then this can be eliminated. Identify enough items/activities so that they can be varied from time to time and day to day. The individual will satiate on items if they are presented continuously. Also, the clinician should periodically conduct further preference assessments to eliminate items that may no longer be preferred and to identify new items/activities. The clinician can use these preferred activities as opportunities to teach participation and to enhance social interactions/social involvement.

Introduce choices

One way to enrich the environment is to provide access to a choice of activities that provide a comparable type of stimulation to the challenging behavior. If a child engages in body rocking, then it may help to get the child to swing in the playground.

Reinforce incompatible behavior

Another strategy for dealing with sensory-motivated challenging behavior is to reinforce incompatible behaviors. If the person engages in finger flicking, then the clinician would find a task that requires the person to use his or her fingers and make sure the person receives reinforcement for this activity. Instead of finger flicking, for example, the person could be reinforced for some functional activities, such as domestic chores (e.g. sweeping, raking, washing clothing).

Summary and conclusion

Behavioral and educational interventions are based on a prior functional assessment of the challenging behavior. Intervention strategies are then selected that match the assessed function of the challenging behavior. Different strategies would be indicated for attention-motivated, tangible-motivated, escape-motivated, and sensory-motivated behaviors.

Underlying effective behavioral and educational interventions are a few basic principles of operant and respondent conditioning as reviewed in Chapter 3. In brief, the basic principles are reinforcement, extinction, and punishment. In practice the basic principles can be translated into a few generic strategies. These generic strategies are: (a) reinforcement is withheld for challenging behavior, (b) reinforcement is delivered for the absence of challenging behavior, on a fixed-time schedule, and contingent on alternative or incompatible behaviors, and (c) when alternative behaviors are absent from the repertoire, educational intervention is needed to teach the individual new responses that will serve as functionally equivalent alternatives to challenging behavior. Effective behavioral and educational intervention requires an understanding of the function of challenging behavior and of the basic operant and respondent principles that shape human behavior.

CHAPTER **8**

Early intervention and prevention

Introduction

In this chapter we consider the theoretical and practical aspects of early intervention for the prevention of challenging behavior in persons with developmental disabilities. Several critical themes will be illustrated in two models that highlight the importance of individualized support and the development of appropriate adaptive behaviors to replace challenging behavior. These themes include the integral relation between increasing adaptive behavior functioning and the amelioration of challenging behavior. In addition, we consider the vital role of family supports and the necessity of considering the contexts in which challenging behaviors occur. After we consider conceptual and research bases our attention will turn to practical issues in early intervention and prevention.

Early intervention

Early intervention is the provision of educational and other supports for young children. In this context young refers to children from birth to about six years of age. Early intervention is intended in part to develop the child's behavioral repertoire and reduce or eliminate challenging behaviors. Early intervention can be highly effective in this respect (Guralnick, 1997), but not all early interventions are effective for all children. At the heart of early intervention for challenging behavior is the prevention of antisocial cycles, which are difficult to break and wide-ranging in terms of their implications for later life. To do so effectively requires interventions that are focused on addressing the factors that have shaped and maintained challenging behavior and teaching specific alternative behaviors to replace challenging behaviors.

With this in mind, one of the central goals of early intervention is the reduction of risk factors for challenging behaviors as discussed in Chapter 2, including the potentially complex and interactive effects of biological factors and health and medical issues with respondent and operant learning processes. Given that communication impairment is characteristic of developmental disability, early intervention that is focused on developing alternative communication skills to replace socially motivated challenging behavior is an important part of prevention. As part of this intervention, there may be a need to create learning environments that are rich in opportunities for communication. Several further examples in this context may be helpful. The early identification of sight or hearing difficulties (or both) enables the child to receive technological and other supports. This may in turn reduce the risk of developing challenging behavior to fill the communicative void. In addition, direct and early instruction to teach turn-taking and sharing might also help prevent the development and persistence of challenging behaviors.

As we noted in Chapter 4, enhancing quality of life and self-determination are critical and central goals in the design of programs to reduce challenging behavior. Restricted life options, limited choice-making opportunities and reduced personal control over the environment might be either the consequence or the cause of challenging behavior. In this chapter, we emphasize the need for the development of adaptive behaviors as a positive means of minimizing the interfering effect of challenging behaviors in the lives of young children with developmental disabilities.

Prevalence

Despite a sizeable body of literature on the prevalence of challenging behaviors (see Chapter 1), there appear to be few studies that have specifically examined the prevalence of challenging behavior in young children. Still, it is possible to make some estimates. In the Isle of Wight study, for example, Michael Rutter (1989) found that students with developmental disabilities were much more likely than their non-disabled peers to display problem behaviors. More specifically, Blackman and Cobb (1988) found that parents of children with developmental disabilities reported higher levels and longer duration of behavioral difficulty in their child's first year of life when compared to the reports of parents of normally developing children. In a statewide study of 78 parents of children with autism and related disabilities, Dunlap, Robbins and Darrow (1994) found that almost 40% of these parents indicated that their child demonstrated frequent challenging behavior (e.g. aggression, pica or self-injury). Although it may not be possible to make too many generalizations from these studies, the results suggest that challenging behavior can begin at a very young age for many individuals with developmental disabilities. Early onset implies the need for early intervention.

Unfortunately many children do not receive effective early intervention to address challenging behaviors. Part of this may stem from the fact
that when challenging behaviors first appear in the repertoires of young
children these acts may not be recognized as a problem that needs treatment. Instead, these behaviors might simply be tolerated in the often
naïve hope they will magically disappear someday. This is understandable. When challenging behaviors first begin in young children they may
be easy to tolerate simply because the child is young and not very strong
and so the aggression or self-injury does not cause much injury or damage.
Hoping and waiting for the child to outgrow the behaviors is also understandable because this sometimes happens in typically developing
children.

Unfortunately, such thinking is mistaken. There is now clear evidence
that once challenging behaviors emerge in children with developmental
disabilities they tend to persist and become worse (Einfeld and Tonge,
1996; Tonge and Einfeld, 1991). As the child develops physically it is also
likely that more injury, damage and disruption will ensue from their acts
of aggression, self-injury and tantrums. Intervening at this point is more
difficult than intervening when the behaviors first appear. Early intervention is therefore necessary. Challenging behavior needs to be nipped in
the bud so to speak. And one way to do this is to implement effective early
intervention to fill the child's repertoire with appropriate alternative
behaviors.

Social competence

Guralnick and Neville (1997) provide a thorough discussion of issues
involved in teaching appropriate adaptive behaviors to young children.
The term social competence is used to describe a well-developed repertoire that includes effective and appropriate behaviors for initiating and
maintaining social interactions with others. These issues are not just
about delivering good instruction, but also include paying attention to
the nature of family dynamics. Definitions of social competence usually
include mention of the milieu of human interaction, including (but not
limited to) dimensions of reciprocity, friendship, and mutual problem
solving in relation to conflict (Guralnick and Neville, 1997). Bearing these
aspects in mind, the human ecology, in all its complexity, is an essential
frame of reference in our analysis of best practice in early intervention to
prevent or reduce challenging behavior, and to facilitate the development
of appropriate adaptive behaviors.

To this end, Figure 8.1 describes the child at the center of a support system that includes parents, peers, and siblings. Based on the ecological

systems approach pioneered by Bronfenbrenner (1979), this schema reminds us of the interplay between critical variables. Each variable impacts, and is potentially impacted by, all others.

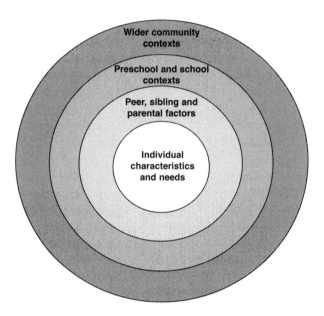

Figure 8.1 An ecological perspective on early intervention to prevent or reduce challenging behavior.

Ecological perspective

Dunlap and Fox (1996) used an ecological perspective in their discussion of the elements of comprehensive support necessary for effective early intervention to reduce and prevent challenging behavior. This chapter draws heavily on their synthesis. In concert with a focus upon individual differences and the various dimensions of adaptive behavior functioning and social competence, best practice and research attention are centered on the inter-related domains of: (a) individual-centered interventions, (b) family-centered interventions, and (c) context-centered interventions (Figure 8.2). In the next section we use these areas as a basis for discussion of the relevant literature. As you review them, you are encouraged to consider the inter-linkages between the individual and the various contextual layers and sources of intervention that surround and impact social behavior (Figures 8.1 and 8.2), as well as the risk factors that we reviewed in Chapter 2.

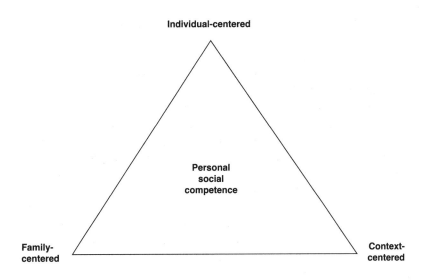

Figure 8.2 Approaches to the development of personal social competence in young children with challenging behaviors.

Individual-centered interventions

A consistent theme in the literature on challenging behavior is the importance of recognizing individual differences in the function or purpose of challenging behavior. Information about the function of a child's challenging behavior is used to select specific adaptive behaviors that might serve as replacements for challenging behavior. As implied by the work of Eric Emerson (1995), part of the aim of early intervention is to develop the child's social competencies by teaching skills that out-compete or will replace challenging behaviors. This precept guides current best practice in the use of functional assessment (see Chapter 6) and more especially, the design and delivery of behavioral and educational treatments (see Chapter 7). Clearly, it is to be hoped that the provision of such supports as early as possible in a child's life will hinder the development of challenging behaviors, and enhance the development of appropriate behaviors (Dunlap, Johnson, and Robbins, 1990; Emerson, 1995; Fox, Dunlap and Powell, 2002; Kiernan, 1994). That is, behavioral and educational interventions should seek to fill the repertoire so that challenging behaviors are neither the only nor the most likely response option.

Three issues are relevant here. The first is the relation and interaction between biological and environmental influences on challenging behavior. It may be important to ask about the nature of the relation between physiological states and learning variables that may set the scene for challenging behaviors. The interested reader is referred to the three-tiered model proposed by Guess and Carr (1991) and a recent study by Reese (1997) in which this model was investigated in relation to the contextual conditions and self-injurious behaviors of a 40-year-old individual with profound mental retardation. In another relevant study, Freeman, Horner and Reichle (1999) explored the relation between heart rate and problem behaviors in two adults with severe disability. Their findings underlined the potential value of including physiological measures in the assessment of challenging behavior. As another example, Ranzon (2001) discussed the nature of the link between anxiety and challenging behavior in people with intellectual disability.

The assessment and treatment of challenging behavior is beginning to become more inter-disciplinary, but all too often the benefits of an inter-disciplinary approach are not realized in early intervention programs. Part of the problem could be the difficulty in putting together an inter-disciplinary team (Orelove and Sobsey, 1996).

A second difficulty sometimes faced by practitioners working with young children with developmental disabilities and challenging behaviors relates to the task of identifying and understanding an individual's bio-behavioral states as was mentioned in Chapter 5. A child's behavioral state might not only influence the extent to which certain environmental variables, such as task demands, affect challenging behavior, but is also likely to influence the effectiveness of interventions that are designed to teach alternative behaviors. Simply put, interventions focused on teaching alternative skills are probably more likely to be effective when the child is in a state of alertness that is conducive to learning.

A third issue to emphasize is the pivotal role of communication intervention as a treatment for challenging behavior. There are several aspects for consideration here. The first of these is the connection between the function of the communication behavior targeted for instruction and the function of the child's challenging behavior. This depends in part on whether the functions of the communication skills targeted for intervention is easily recognized by the child's listeners. It also depends on whether the newly acquired communication skills are more efficient at recruiting reinforcement than challenging behavior. Both of these factors contribute to the test of functional equivalence: A test that must be passed to increase the likelihood of intervention success. The test of functional equivalence examines whether the alternative behavior does in fact serve the same function as the child's challenging behavior (Mirenda, 1997).

In a classic early example of this approach, Carr and Durand (1985) taught four young children with developmental disabilities a variety of ways of obtaining assistance and attention after they had established that their aggressive and self-injurious behaviors were serving to communicate such functions. By successfully replacing inappropriate behaviors with skills that achieved the same purposes, Carr and Durand stimulated a research and practice agenda that has spanned two decades (see Mirenda, 1997) and continues to evolve in the broader processes of functional assessment and positive behavior support. The issue of relevance for this chapter is whether early intervention to teach functional communication skills would effectively prevent the emergence and persistence of challenging behavior in children with developmental disabilities who are at risk of developing challenging behaviors. Few studies have involved children young enough to explore this issue.

One relevant study was reported by Arndorfer et al. (1994). In this study, two students with developmental delays and challenging behaviors received communication intervention in the home. The first child (a 3-year-old) was taught to request attention without hitting or kicking. The other child, a 2-year-old with self-injurious head banging, was taught a more appropriate means of requesting access to preferred objects (i.e. a toy). The selection of these communication skills was based on the hypotheses that the hitting and kicking for child 1 was maintained by positive reinforcement in the form of contingent adult attention, whereas child 2's self-injury was maintained by positive reinforcement in the form of gaining access to tangible objects such as toys. The hypotheses appeared to be good ones because there was a decrease in challenging behavior for both children as they acquired the replacement communication skills.

A second area of emphasis in relation to communication processes has been the translation of empirical findings and best practice recommendations into everyday contexts, including the family home, pre-schools and educational programs (Arthur, Butterfield and McKinnon, 1998; Butterfield et al., 1995; Stephenson and Dowrick, 2000). Current state-of-the-art practices in early intervention involve a number of components, including: (a) using multiple sources of assessment data to develop intervention goals, (b) using typical daily activities (such as play, mealtimes and self-care routines) as the context for intervention, (c) providing numerous opportunities for learning and for building fluency of newly acquired skills, and (d) including procedures to promote maintenance and generalization of skill gains (Duker et al., in press). In addition, a number of writers have suggested that embedding learning opportunities into naturally emerging situations may lead to enhanced generalization and spontaneity, and perhaps most importantly it might also allow for increased choice-making (Brown et al., 1998; Brown and Lehr, 1993; Siegel-Causey and Bashinski, 1997).

For young children, play is seen as a natural and developmentally appropriate setting for implementing early intervention. However the important point is intervention should occur in the same contexts in which challenging behavior is a problem. If tantrums occur during play routines, then intervention to teach alternatives to challenging behavior should occur during play routines. On the other hand, if challenging behaviors occur during other activities, such as mealtimes, bedtimes, grocery shopping or transitions in the school, then the intervention procedures to teach alternatives to challenging behavior should occur in these settings and should not simply be limited to play. The basic principle is to always intervene in the situation where the problem occurs.

At a broader level, discussion of individual-centered interventions for young children with developmental disability and challenging behavior would be incomplete without attention to the work of Lovaas and his colleagues. Lovaas has reported dramatic improvements in the IQ and adaptive behavior functioning in children with autism following intensive behavioral intervention (for example, Lovaas, 1987; McEachlin, Smith and Lovaas, 1993). In addition, several replication studies have broadly supported these findings (Anderson et al., 1987; Birnbrauer and Leach, 1993), although not always with such dramatic improvements.

In a recent well-controlled study that reflected the principles and practices of the original Lovaas studies, Smith, Groen and Wynn (2000) compared intensive behavioral treatment (e.g. 25 hours/week of training over several years) to a less intensive and shorter (3–9 month) parent-training program. They found that for children with autism and those with pervasive developmental disorder not otherwise specified (PDD/NOS), the intensive intervention produced higher gains in language and IQ scores than did the parent training program. However, there were no significant post-intervention differences for the two groups in terms of overall adaptive/social behavior functioning. Despite a number of acknowledged constraints, and modest results when compared with the earlier findings of Lovaas and others, this study provides further evidence of the value of intensive early and behaviorally based interventions for young children with developmental disabilities.

Our reading of the literature is that behavioral and educational interventions are the only effective interventions for young children with autism and related developmental disabilities. This does not mean that all interventions that are touted as behavioral or educational are the same and will therefore be effective. Rather it means that interventions based on empirically validated principles of learning (e.g. operant and respondent conditioning) have consistently demonstrated their effectiveness; whereas other treatments, such as medications, sensory integration, gentle teaching, and facilitated communication (the list of unproven treatments could go on and on) have no such history of demonstrated effectiveness. However, as we have noted (Figure 8.1), behavioral and educational interventions can be enhanced and complemented by including a focus on family-centered practices.

Family-centered interventions

An increasing amount of research attention is being paid to the experiences and needs of families of children with developmental disabilities (Ellis et al., 2002; Heiman, 2002), including the siblings of children with developmental disabilities (Cuskelly, Chant and Hayes, 1998), parental stress in relation to child behavior problems (Hastings, 2002), and the impact of problem behavior on overall family processes and dynamics (Fox et al., 2002). Consider the work of Fox et al. (2002), who interviewed 20 family members of children (aged 3–12 years). All the children had developmental disabilities and challenging behavior and all of the families were involved in a program offering family-centered positive behavior support. The results indicated that families valued supports beyond just effective early intervention to teach skills to the child. This suggests that it will be important to develop behaviorally based interventions focused on teaching adaptive behaviors to the child in the overall context of a system of family supports.

Current literature on early intervention reflects an emphasis on the overlapping roles of families, researchers, and service providers in a shared, collaborative and supportive partnership. In true collaboration, the input of all participants is valued and used in the design of individually appropriate programs. For example, intervention to teach communication skills to replace challenging behaviors can include providing a pivotal role for family members who may need support so that they can learn how to respond to the child's newly acquired augmentative communication skills, for example. In contrast to exclusive use of a one-to-one training format in a clinic room by a speech pathologist, an approach that included the family would have more ecological validity and this, in turn, may promote generalization and maintenance.

Parents are critical agents of change, but may require support to be effective change agents. Along these lines, the use of Parent Management Training (PMT) can be effective. PMT involves the use of role plays, discussion, and modeling to teach parents the skills necessary to implement effective behavioral and educational interventions (Lutzker and Steed, 1998). Parents can be taught how to identify problem behaviors and implement strategies to teach adaptive behaviors and reduce challenging behaviors. Robbins and Dunlap (1992), for example, worked with 15 autistic children who were 2–5 years of age. They taught the mothers of these children how to implement training programs for teaching adaptive behaviors. Parent training involved telling the parents how to use the teaching procedures, showing the parents how to implement the procedures, and then providing feedback as the parents practiced implementing the techniques. The results showed that the parent's teaching skills improved and this led to reductions in the child's challenging behaviors. This is the type of support that parents find valuable.

In another relevant project, Wacker et al. (1996) provided a comprehensive model for developing and maintaining long-term reciprocal positive relationships between parents and their children with challenging behavior. Wacker et al. (1996) began the process with a functional analysis of the child's challenging behavior. This was followed by an intervention that was intended to replace challenging behavior by teaching functionally equivalent communication skills. Throughout this process, parents were involved as active collaborators. Ongoing data analysis, as described in Chapter 7, was used to guide decision-making about whether the intervention was working or needed to be revised. Most impressively, maintenance and generalization were planned for from the outset of intervention by teaching key or pivotal responses that will lead to reinforcement for the child. Their data suggest that parents can be included as clinicians in early intervention for challenging behavior and one way to include them that is meaningful is to teach the parents how to use effective, evidence-based intervention procedures based on empirically validated principles of learning. This is consistent with the theory outlined in Chapter 3 that challenging behaviors are shaped by consequences and persist in part because the child's overall behavioral repertoire is restricted.

Context-centered interventions

The context of intervention includes a consideration of where the intervention occurs. An intervention is ecologically valid to the extent that it is conducted in the everyday contexts where the child lives, attends school and participates in the community. The overall aim of early intervention is to increase participation in typical home, school and community environments. This is often referred to as inclusion.

Inclusive contexts can be used as a means of teaching and supporting appropriate social skills in young children with developmental disabilities (Strain, McGee and Kohler, 2000). Examples of these inclusive contexts include preschools that enrol students with and without disabilities as well as early intervention programs in local schools or integrated centers. In his discussion of 27 years of research and work with young children with autism, Strain (2001) noted that "Access to more inclusive settings for young children with autism can represent access to the most effective intervention strategies for addressing the core social deficit of autism" (p. 31).

When we contrast inclusive settings with segregated situations serving young children with behavioral needs, is it possible to define some of the critical variables that facilitate behavior change? Strain and his colleagues have explored this area in depth and the interested reader should review Strain (2001) for a valuable synthesis of lessons learned from a career of research in this area. He points to the central importance of understanding the nature of social exchanges involving children with disabilities and those without, and most especially, the duration and reciprocity of such exchanges. For a friendship to blossom, it may require opportunities for the child to develop a relationships with other children. To do this it may be helpful to ensure the child learns social skills that will endear them to their peers. This often requires intervention to teach skills such as sharing toys, helping others when they need help, and showing affection to peers when appropriate (Strain, 2001). Peer modeling can be an important aspect of inclusive programming, and can be usefully accompanied by the positive reinforcement of children who act as exemplars of social interaction. The idea here is that as the child acquires more friends and more friendship skills, challenging behaviors directed at peers would be expected to show a collateral decrease.

Peer training is one strategy that has been used in inclusive situations as a means of shaping social skills so as to foster friendships between children with and without developmental disabilities. Typically, play serves as the context for this type of shaping program (Arthur, Bochner and Butterfield, 1999). Considerable evidence now exists demonstrating the efficacy of this type of peer training, both in terms of the benefits for the child with developmental disability and the benefits for nonhandicapped peers (Strain, 2001; Strain and Kohler, 1998).

Beyond these educational contexts, inclusion and participation in the wider community can also provide a broad platform for the development of adaptive behavior that may help to increase the options in the child's repertoire so that challenging behaviors become a less likely response (Dunlap and Fox, 1996). Although acquisition of new skills can often be effectively undertaken in structured one-to-one teaching environments (Duker et al., in press), the use of additional environments may enhance generalization of newly acquired skills. Thus behavioral interventions to replace challenging behavior might be conducted in numerous settings, but at some point there is the need to ensure the gains are maintained in all of the settings that the child and his or her family access.

Implications for service delivery and practice

Throughout the research we have reviewed above and the frames of reference provided in Figures 8.1 and 8.2, four implications emerge. First, there is a considerable body of evidence to show that early intervention can be effective in developing adaptive behaviors and reducing challenging behaviors. Such interventions may even help to prevent challenging behaviors in some cases if they are provided early enough. Accordingly, early and effective behavioral intervention needs to occur as soon as possible.

A second, related implication is that the most effective interventions to date are characterized by intensive behavioral and educational interventions focused on teaching a range of adaptive behaviors and functionally equivalent alternatives to challenging behavior. Behavioral and educational interventions are enhanced by adopting an interdisciplinary approach that involves the parents as collaborators (Golly et al., 2000).

Third, it is critical to monitor the effectiveness of interventions and make adjustments as necessary (Wacker et al., 1996). This requires an approach to intervention that is flexible and responsive to the child's behavior. This cannot be achieved by blindly following a set curriculum or procedures. Rather it requires an understanding of the basic operant and respondent principles (see Chapter 3) that underlie effective intervention. Strain (2001) supports this need for flexibility by observing that the peer-mediated approach he uses works only "when the intervention is tweaked to meet idiosyncratic needs" (p. 35).

Fourth, Figures 8.1 and 8.2 illustrate the complex human ecologies commonly experienced by children with developmental disabilities and challenging behaviors. Given this complexity, support for families and children will need to be ongoing.

Summary and conclusion

In this chapter, we considered several critical aspects of early intervention in the prevention and treatment of challenging behavior. Figures 8.1 and 8.2 were introduced as a means of exploring the ecological connection among variables that impact on the effectiveness of early intervention services, and the central goal of increasing the child's behavioral repertoire in intervention. An effective early intervention would be one that addressed the risk factors outlined in Chapter 2 and involved a thorough medical screening (Chapter 5) and a functional assessment of the challenging behavior (Chapter 6). Early intervention would then focus on resolving any identified medical problems and developing the child's overall behavioral repertoire by teaching alternative adaptive behaviors, as well as implementing treatment strategies matched to the function of the child's challenging behaviors (Chapter 7). Early intervention is critical, but its effectiveness depends on the clinician's ability to consider risk factors within a sound theory of challenging behavior (Chapters 2 and 3). Finally, early intervention for the treatment and prevention of challenging behavior is enhanced by interventions that cover individual, family, and contextual factors as discussed in this chapter.

References

Abang TB (1985) Blindism: likely causes and preventative measures. Journal of Visual Impairment & Blindness 79: 400–1.

Alberto PA, Troutman AC (1999) Applied Behavior Analysis for Teachers (5th edn). Columbus, OH: Merrill.

Aman MG, Sarphare G, Burrow W (1995) Psychoactive drugs in group homes: prevalence and relation to demographic/psychiatric variables. American Journal of Mental Retardation 99: 500–9.

American Psychiatric Association (1994) Diagnostic and Statistical Manual of Mental Disorders (4th edn). Washington DC: APA.

Anderson SR, Avery DL, DiPietro EK et al. (1987) Intensive home-based intervention with autistic children. Education and Treatment of Children 10: 352–66.

Arndorfer RE, Miltenberger RG, Woster SH et al. (1994) Home-based descriptive and experimental analysis of problem behaviors in children. Topics in Early Childhood Special Education 14(1): 64–87.

Artesani JA, Mallar L (1998) Positive behavior supports in general education settings: combining person-centered planning and functional analysis. Intervention in School and Clinic 34: 33–40.

Arthur M, Bochner S, Butterfield N (1999) Enhancing peer interactions within the context of play. International Journal of Disability, Development and Education 46: 367–81.

Arthur M, Butterfield N, MacKinnon D (1998) Communication intervention for students with severe disability: results of a partner training program. International Journal of Disability, Development and Education 45: 97–115.

Arthur M, Bruveris I, Smith G, Stephenson-Roberts V (2002) A NSW example of professional development in the design of effective behaviour support plans. Special Education Perspectives 11(1): 51–8.

Bailey JS (1992) Gentle teaching: trying to win friends and influence people with euphemism, metaphor, smoke, and mirrors. Journal of Applied Behavior Analysis 25: 879–83.

Bailey JS, Pyles AM (1989) Behavioral diagnostics. In E Cipani (ed.), The Treatment of Severe Behavior Disorders: Behavior Analysis Approaches. Monographs of the American Association on Mental Retardation, No. 12 (pp. 85–107). Washington, DC: American Association on Mental Retardation.

Bak S (1999) Relationships between inappropriate behaviors and other factors in young children with visual impairments. Review 31: 84–91.

Batshaw ML (ed.) (1997) Children with Disabilities (4th edn). Baltimore: Paul H. Brookes Publishing Co.

Beange H (1987) Our client's health: their responsibility or ours? Australia and New Zealand Journal of Developmental Disabilities 13: 175–7.

Beitchman JH, Peterson M (1986) Disorders of language, communication, and behavior in mentally retarded children: some ideas on their co-occurrence. Psychiatric Clinics of North America 9: 689–98.

Berkson G, Davenport RK (1962) Stereotyped movements of mental defectives. I. Initial survey. American Journal of Mental Deficiency 66: 849–52.

Berkson G, Rafaeli-Mor N, Tarnovsky S (1999) Body-rocking and other habits of college students and persons with mental retardation. American Journal on Mental Retardation 104: 107–16.

Bettelheim B (1949) Harry – a study in rehabilitation. Journal of Abnormal and Social Psychology 44: 231–65.

Bettelheim B (1955) Truants from Life: The Rehabilitation of Emotionally Disturbed Children. New York: The Free Press.

Bettelheim B (1974) A Home for the Heart. New York: Knopf.

Birnbrauer JS, Leach DJ (1993) The Murdoch early intervention program after 2 years. Behaviour Change 10: 63–74.

Blackman JA, Cobb LS (1988) A comparison of parent's perceptions of common behavior problems in developmentally at risk and normal children. Child Health Care 18: 108–13.

Blatt B, Kaplan F (1974) Christmas in Purgatory: A Photographic Essay on Mental Retardation. Syracuse, NY: Human Policy Press.

Borthwick-Duffy SA (1994) Prevalence of destructive behaviors. In T Thompson, DB Gray (eds), Destructive Behavior in Developmental Disabilities: Diagnosis and Treatment (pp. 3–23). Thousand Oaks, CA: Sage.

Bosch J, Van Dyke DC, Smith S, Poulton S (1997) Role of medical conditions in the exacerbation of self-injurious behavior: an exploratory study. Mental Retardation 35: 124–30.

Bronfenbrenner U (1979) The Ecology of Human Development: Experiments by Nature and Design. Cambridge, MA: Harvard University Press.

Browder DM (2001) Curriculum and Assessment for Students with Moderate and Severe Disabilities. New York: The Guilford Press.

Brown F, Lehr D (1993) Making activities meaningful for students with severe multiple disabilities. Teaching Exceptional Children 25(4): 12–16.

Brown F, Gothelf CR, Guess D, Lehr DH (1998) Self-determination for individuals with the most severe disabilities: moving beyond chimera. Journal of the Association for Persons with Severe Handicaps 23: 17–26.

Butterfield N, Arthur M, Sigafoos J (1995) Partners in Everyday Communicative Exchanges: A Guide to Promoting Interaction Involving People with Severe Intellectual Disability. Baltimore: Paul H. Brookes Publishing Co.

Carlson G (2002) Supporting the health and well-being of people with intellectual disability and high support needs through networking and resource development. Australian Occupational Therapy Journal 49: 37–43.

Carr EG (1977) The motivation of self-injurious behavior: a review of some hypotheses. Psychological Bulletin 84: 800–16.

Carr EG, Durand VM (1985) Reducing behavior problems through functional communication training. Journal of Applied Behavior Analysis 18: 111–26.

Carr EG, McDowell JJ (1980) Social control of self-injurious behavior of organic etiology. Behavior Therapy 11: 402–9.

Carr EG, Smith CE (1995) Biological setting events for self-injury. Mental Retardation and Developmental Disabilities Research Reviews 12: 94–98.

Carr EG, Dunlap G, Horner RH et al. (2002) Positive behavior support: evolution of an applied science. Journal of Positive Behavior Interventions 4: 4–16.

Carr EG, Levin L, McConnachie G et al. (1994) Communication-based Intervention for Problem Behavior. Baltimore: Paul H. Brookes Publishing Co.

Cataldo MF, Harris J (1982) The biological basis for self-injury in the mentally retarded. Analysis and Intervention in Developmental Disabilities 2: 21–39.

Chamberlain L, Chung MC, Jenner L (1993) Preliminary findings on communication and challenging behaviour in learning difficulty. British Journal of Developmental Disabilities 39: 118–25.

Chan JB, Sigafoos J (2000) A review of child and family characteristics related to the use of respite care in developmental disability services. Child & Youth Care Forum 29: 27–37.

Chandler LK (2000) A training and consultation model to reduce resistance and increase educator knowledge and skill in addressing challenging behaviours. Special Education Perspectives 9: 3–13.

Chandler LK, Dahlquist CM, Repp AC, Feltz C (1999) The effects of team-based functional assessment on the behavior of students in classroom settings. Exceptional Children 66: 101–22.

Chung MC, Bickerton W, Cumella S, Winchester C (1996) A preliminary study on the prevalence of challenging behaviours. Psychological Reports 79: 1427–30.

Clarke DJ, Boer H (1998) Problem behaviors associated with deletion Prader-Willi, Smith-Magenis, and Cri du Chat syndromes. American Journal on Mental Retardation 103: 264–71.

Cummins RA (1991) The Comprehensive Quality of Life Scale – Intellectual Disability: an instrument under development. Australia and New Zealand Journal of Developmental Disabilities 17: 259–64.

Cuskelly M, Chant D, Hayes A (1998) Behaviour problems in the siblings of children with Down syndrome: associations with family responsibilities and parental stress. International Journal of Disability, Development and Education 45: 295–311.

De Lissovoy V (1963) Head banging in early childhood: a suggested cause. Journal of Genetic Psychology 102: 109–14.

DePaepe P, Shores R, Jack S (1996) Effects of task difficulty on the on-task behavior of students with severe behavior disorders. Behavioral Disorders 21: 216–25.

Didden R, Sigafoos J (2001) A review of the nature and treatment of sleep disorders in individuals with developmental disabilities. Research in Developmental Disabilities 22: 255–72.

Didden R, Duker P, Korzilius H (1997) Meta-analytic study of treatment effectiveness for problem behaviors with individuals who have mental retardation. American Journal on Mental Retardation 101: 387–99.

Drasgow E, Yell ML (2001) Functional behavioral assessments: legal requirements and challenges. School Psychology Review 30(2): 239–51.

Duker PC, Didden R, Sigafoos J (in press) One-to-one Training: Instructional Procedures for Learners with Developmental Disabilities. Austin, TX: Pro-Ed.

Duncan D, Matson JL, Bamburg JW et al. (1999) The relationship of self-injurious behavior and aggression to social skills in persons with severe and profound learning disability. Research in Developmental Disabilities 20: 441–8.

Dunlap G, Fox L (1996) Early intervention and serious problem behaviours: a comprehensive approach. In LK Koegel, RL Koegel, G Dunlap (eds), Positive Behavioral Support: Including People with Difficult Behavior in the Community (pp. 31–50). Baltimore: Paul H. Brookes.

Dunlap G, Johnson IF, Robbins FR (1990) Preventing serious behavior problems through skill development and early interventions. In AC Repp, NN Singh (eds), Perspectives on the Use of Nonaversive and Aversive Interventions for Persons with Developmental Disabilities (pp. 273–86). Sycamore, IL: Sycamore Publishing Co.

Dunlap G, Robbins FR, Darrow MA (1994) Parents' reports of their children's challenging behaviors: results of a statewide survey. Mental Retardation 32: 206–12.

Dunne RG, Asher KN, Rivara FP (1993) Injuries in young people with developmental disabilities: comparative investigations from the 1988 National Health Interview Survey. Mental Retardation 31: 83–8.

Durand VM, Crimmins DB (1988) Identifying the variables maintaining self-injurious behavior. Journal of Autism & Developmental Disorders 18: 99–117.

Durand VM, Crimmins DB (1991) Teaching functionally equivalent responses as an intervention for challenging behavior. In B Remington (ed.), The Challenge of Severe Mental Handicap: A Behavior Analytic Approach (pp. 71–95). Chichester: John Wiley & Sons.

Einfeld SL (1992) Clinical assessment of psychiatric symptoms in mentally retarded individuals. Australia and New Zealand Journal of Psychiatry 26: 48–63.

Einfeld SL, Aman M (1995) Issues in the taxonomy of psychopathology in mental retardation. Journal of Autism and Developmental Disorders 25: 143–67.

Einfeld SL, Tonge BJ (1996) Population prevalence of psychopathology in children and adolescents with intellectual disability: II. Epidemiological findings. Journal of Intellectual Disability Research 40: 99–109.

Ellis JT, Luiselli JK, Amirault D et al. (2002) Families of children with developmental disabilities: assessment and comparison of self-reported needs in relation to situational variables. Journal of Developmental and Physical Disabilities 14: 191–202.

Emerson E (1995) Challenging Behaviour: Analysis and Intervention in People with Learning Disabilities. Cambridge: Cambridge University Press.

Emerson E, Cummins R, Barrett S et al. (1988) Challenging behaviour and community services: 2. Who are the people who challenge services? Mental Handicap 16: 16–19.

Emerson E, Kiernan C, Alborz A et al. (2001) The prevalence of challenging behaviors: a total population study. Research in Developmental Disabilities 22: 77–93.

Evenhuis H, Henderson CM, Beange H et al. (2001) Healthy ageing adults with intellectual disabilities: physical health issues. Journal of Applied Research in Intellectual Disabilities 14: 175–94.

Ferster CB, Skinner BF (1957) Schedules of Reinforcement. New York: Appleton-Century-Crofts.

Fox L, Dunlap G, Powell D (2002) Young children with challenging behavior: issues and considerations for behavior support. Journal of Positive Behavior Interventions 4: 208–18.

Fox L, Vaughn BJ, Wyatte ML, Dunlap G (2002) "We can't expect other people to understand": family perspectives on problem behavior. Exceptional Children 68: 437–50.

Fraser S (1995) The Bell Curve Wars: Race, Intelligence, and the Future of America. New York: Basic Books.

Freeman RL, Horner RH, Reichle J (1999) Relation between heart rate and problem behaviors. American Journal on Mental Retardation 104: 330–45.

Gabler-Halle D, Halle JW, Chung YB (1993) The effects of aerobic exercise on psychological and behavioral variables of individuals with developmental disabilities: a critical review. Research in Developmental Disabilities 14: 359–86.

Gardner W, Cole C, Davidson D, Karan O (1986) Reducing aggression in individuals with developmental disabilities: an expanded stimulus control, assessment, and intervention model. Education and Training of the Mentally Retarded 21: 3–12.

Gedye A (1989) Episodic rage and aggression attributed to frontal lobe seizures. Journal of Mental Deficiency Research 33: 369–79.

Gillberg C, O'Brien G (eds) (2000) Developmental Disability and Behaviour. London: MacKeith Press.

Golly A, Sprague J, Walker H et al. (2000) The first step to success program: an analysis of outcomes with identical twins across multiple baselines. Behavioral Disorders 25: 170–82.

Graziano AM (2002) Developmental Disabilities: Introduction to a Diverse Field. Boston: Allyn & Bacon.

Griffin JC, Ricketts RW, Williams DE et al. (1987) A community survey of self-injurious behavior among developmentally disabled children and adolescents. Hospital and Community Psychiatry 38: 959–63.

Guess D, Carr E (1991) Emergence and maintenance of stereotypy and self-injury. American Journal on Mental Retardation 96: 299–326.

Guess D, Roberts S, Siegel-Causey E et al. (1993) Analysis of behavior state conditions and associated environmental variables among students with profound handicaps. American Journal on Mental Retardation 97: 634–53.

Gunsett RP, Mulick JA, Fernald WB, Martin JL (1989) Indications for medical screening prior to behavioral programming for severely and profoundly mentally retarded clients. Journal of Autism and Developmental Disorders 19: 167–72.

Guralnick MJ (1997) The Effectiveness of Early Intervention. Baltimore: Paul H. Brookes.

Guralnick MJ, Neville B (1997) Designing early intervention programs to promote children's social competence. In MJ Guralnick (ed.), The Effectiveness of Early Intervention. Baltimore: Paul H. Brookes.

Hall S, Oliver C, Murphy G (2001) Early development of self-injurious behavior: an empirical study. American Journal on Mental Retardation 106: 189–99.

Haring TG, Kennedy C (1990) Contextual control of problem behavior in students with severe disabilities. Journal of Applied Behavior Analysis 23: 235–43.

Hastings RP (2002) Parental stress and behaviour problems of children with developmental disability. Journal of Intellectual and Developmental Disability 27: 149–60.

Hawkins R, Dobes R (1975) Behavioral definitions in applied behavior analysis: explicit or implicit. In B Etzel, J LeBlanc, D Baer (eds), New Developments in Behavioral Research: Theory, Methods, and Applications: In Honor of Sidney W. Bijou (pp. 167–88). Hillsdale, NJ: Erlbaum.

Heckaman K, Conroy M, Fox J, Chait A (2000) Functional assessment-based intervention research on students with or at risk for emotional and behavioral disorders in school settings. Behavioral Disorders 25: 196–210.

Heiman T (2002) Parents of children with disabilities: resilience, coping, and future expectations. Journal of Developmental and Physical Disabilities 14: 159–71.

Helm JM, Simeonsson RJ (1989) Assessment of behavioral state organization. In DB Bailey, M Wolery (eds), Assessing Infants and Preschoolers with Handicaps (pp. 202–24). Columbus, OH: Merrill.

Herrnstein RJ (1970) On the law of effect. Journal of the Experimental Analysis of Behavior 13: 243–66.

Herrnstein RJ, Murray C (1994) The Bell Curve: Intelligence and Class Structure in American Life. New York: Free Press.

Hibbins R, Compton D (1994) Measuring Quality of Life: A Person of Place Focus. Paper presented at the Conference of the Australian Association for Social Research, Launceston, Tasmania.

Hill BK, Bruininks RH (1984) Maladaptive behavior of mentally retarded individuals in residential facilities. American Journal of Mental Deficiency 88: 380–7.

Hillery J (1999) Self-injurious behaviour and people with developmental disability. In N Bouras (ed.), Psychiatric and Behavioural Disorders in Developmental Disabilities and Mental Retardation (pp. 109–20). New York: Cambridge University Press.

Holburn S, Vietze PM (eds) (2002) Person-centred Planning: Changing Lives through Research. Baltimore: Paul H. Brookes Publishing Co.

Holloway JB, Sigafoos J (1999) Quality of life for young adults with mental retardation in open versus sheltered employment. European Journal on Mental Disability 5: 13–25.

Horner RD (1980) The effects of an environmental "enrichment" program on the behavior of institutionalized profoundly retarded children. Journal of Applied Behavior Analysis 13(3): 473–91.

Horner RH (2000) Positive behavior supports. Focus on Autism and Other Developmental Disabilities 15: 97–105.

Horner RH, Diemer SM, Brazeau KC (1992) Educational support for students with severe problem behaviors in Oregon: a descriptive analysis from the 1987–1988 school year. Journal of the Association for Persons with Severe Handicaps 17(3): 154–69.

Iwata B, Dorsey M, Slifer K et al. (1982) Toward a functional analysis of self-injury. Analysis and Intervention in Developmental Disabilities 2: 3–20. Reprinted in Journal of Applied Behavior Analysis (1994) 27: 197–209.

Iwata B, Pace G, Dorsey M et al. (1994) The functions of self-injurious behavior: an experimental-epidemiological analysis. Journal of Applied Behavior Analysis 27: 215–40.

Jackson L, Panyan MV (2002) Positive Behavioral Support in the Classroom: Principles and Practices. Baltimore: Paul H. Brookes Publishing Co.

Jacobson JW (1982) Problem behavior and psychiatric impairment within a developmentally disabled population. I: Behavior frequency. Applied Research in Mental Retardation 3: 121–39.

Jacobson JW (1990) Assessing the prevalence of psychiatric disorders in a developmentally population. In E Dibble, DB Grey (eds), Assessment of Behavior Problems with Persons with Mental Retardation Living in the Community (pp. 19–70). Rockville, MD: Department of Health and Human Services, National Institutes of Health, Public Health Services, Alcohol, Drug Abuse, and Mental Health Administration.

Jacobson JW, Mulick JA, Schwartz AA (1995) A history of facilitated communication: science, pseudoscience, and anti-science. American Psychologist 50: 750–65.

Janicki MP, Davidson PW, Henderson CM et al. (2002) Health characteristics and health services utilization in older adults with intellectual disability living in community residences. Journal of Intellectual Disability Research 46: 287–98.

Journal of Applied Behavior Analysis (1968–present) Bloomington, IL: Society for the Experimental Analysis of Behavior.

Journal of the Experimental Analysis of Behavior (1958–present) Bloomington, IL: Society for the Experimental Analysis of Behavior.

Kearney CA, Durand VM, Mindell JA (1995) Choice assessment in residential settings. Journal of Developmental & Physical Disabilities 7: 203–13.

Kennedy C, Itkonen T (1993) Effects of setting events on the problem behavior of students with severe disabilities. Journal of Applied Behavior Analysis 26: 321–7.

Kennedy CH, Meyer KA (1996) Sleep deprivation, allergy symptoms, and negatively reinforced challenging behavior. Journal of Applied Behavior Analysis 29: 133–5.

Kennedy CH, Meyer KA (1998) The use of psychotropic medication for people with severe disabilities and challenging behavior: current status and future directions. Journal of the Association for Persons with Severe Handicaps 23: 83–97.

Kerbeshian J, Burd L, Avery K (2001) Pharmacotherapy of autism: a review and clinical approach. Journal of Developmental and Physical Disabilities 13: 199–227.

Kiernan C (1994) Early Intervention and Challenging Behaviour. Manchester: Hester Adrian Research Centre, University of Manchester.

Kiernan C, Qureshi H (1993) Challenging behaviour. In C Kiernan (ed.), Research to Practice? Implications of Research on Challenging Behavior of People with Learning Disability (pp. 53–65). Clevedon, Avon: British Institute on Learning Disabilities Publications.

Kiernan C, Reeves D, Alborz A (1995) The use of anti-psychotic drugs with adults with learning disabilities and challenging behaviour. Journal of Intellectual Disability Research 39: 263–74.

Kincaid D, Knoster T, Harrower JK et al. (2002) Measuring the impact of positive behavior support. Journal of Positive Behavior Interventions 4: 109–17.

Larson PJ, Maag JW (1998) Applying functional assessment in general educational classrooms: issues and recommendations. Remedial and Special Education 19(6): 338–49.

Lee VL (1988) Beyond Behaviorism. Hillsdale, NJ: Lawrence Erlbaum.

Lehr DH, Brown F (eds) (1996) People with Disabilities who Challenge the System. Baltimore: Paul H. Brookes Publishing Co.

Lennox N, Chaplin R (1995) The psychiatric care of people with intellectual disabilities: the perceptions of trainee psychiatrists and psychiatric medical officers. Australia & New Zealand Journal of Psychiatry 29: 632–7.

Lennox N, Chaplin R (1996) The psychiatric care of people with intellectual disabilities: the perceptions of consultant psychiatrists in Victoria. Australia & New Zealand Journal of Psychiatry 30: 774–80.

Lennox N, Diggens J (1999a) Knowledge, skills and attitudes: medical schools' coverage of an ideal curriculum on intellectual disability. Journal of Intellectual Disability Research 24: 341–7.

Lennox N, Diggens J (1999b) Medical education and intellectual disability: a survey of Australian medical schools. Journal of Intellectual and Developmental Disability 24: 333–40.

Lennox, N., Diggens J, Ugoni A (1997) The general practice care of people with intellectual disability: barriers and solutions. Journal of Intellectual Disability Research 41: 380–90.

Lennox N, Diggens J, Ugoni A (2000) Health care for people with an intellectual disability: general practitioners' attitudes, and provision of care. Journal of Intellectual and Developmental Disability 25: 127–33.

Lennox N, Green M, Diggens J, Ugoni A (2001) Audit and comprehensive health assessment programme in the primary healthcare of adults with intellectual disability: a pilot study. Journal of Intellectual Disability Research 45: 226–32.

Lesch M, Nyhan WI (1964) A familial disorder of uric acid metabolism and central nervous system function. American Journal of Medicine 36: 561.

Lovaas OI (1987) Behavioral treatment and normal education and intellectual functioning in young autistic children. Journal of Consulting and Clinical Psychology 55: 3–9.

Lovaas OI, Simmons TQ (1969) Manipulation of self-destruction in three retarded children. Journal of Applied Behavior Analysis 2: 143–57.

Lovaas OI, Newsom C, Hickman C (1987) Self-stimulatory behavior and perceptual reinforcement. Journal of Applied Behavior Analysis 20: 45–68.

Lovaas OI, Ackerman AB, Alexander D et al. (1981) Teaching Developmentally Disabled Children: The ME Book. Austin, TX: Pro-Ed.

Lovaas OI, Freitag G, Gold VJ, Kassorla IC (1965) Experimental studies in childhood schizophrenia: analysis of self-destructive behavior. Journal of Experimental Child Psychology 2: 67–84.

Lowe K, Felce D (1995) How do carers assess the severity of challenging behaviour? A total population study. Journal of Intellectual Disability Research 39: 117–29.

Lowry MA, Sovner R (1992) Severe behaviour problems associated with rapid cycling bipolar disorder in two adults with profound mental retardation. Journal of Intellectual Disability Research 36: 269–81.

Luckasson R, Coulter DL, Polloway EA et al. (1992) Mental Retardation: Definition, Classification, and Systems of Support (9th edn). Washington, DC: American Association on Mental Retardation.

Luiselli JK, Blew P, Keane J et al. (2000) Pharmacotherapy for severe aggression in a child with autism: "open label" evaluation of multiple medications on response frequency and intensity of behavioral intervention. Journal of Behaviour Therapy and Experimental Psychiatry 31: 219–30.

Lutzker JR, Steed SE (1998) Parent training for families of children with developmental disabilities. In JM Briemeister, CE Schaefer (eds), Handbook of Parent Training. Parents as Co-therapists for Children's Behavior Problems (2nd edn) (pp. 281–307). New York: John Wiley & Sons.

Maag JW (2000) Managing resistance. Intervention in School and Clinic 35: 131–40.

Maag JW (2001) Rewarded by punishment: reflections on the disuse of positive reinforcement in schools. Exceptional Children 67: 173–86.

McEachlin JJ, Smith T, Lovaas OI (1993) Long-term outcome for children with autism who received early intensive behavioral treatment. American Journal on Mental Retardation 97: 359–73.

McGee JJ (1992) Gentle teaching's assumptions and paradigm. Journal of Applied Behavior Analysis 25: 869–72.

McGrew K, Bruininks RH (1989) The factor structure of adaptive behavior. School Psychology Review 18: 64–81.

Magito-McLaughlin D, Mullen-James K, Anderson-Ryan K, Carr EG (2002) Best practices: finding a new direction for Christos. Journal of Positive Behavior Interventions 4: 156–64.

Matson JL, Barrett RP (eds) (1993) Psychopathology in the Mentally Retarded (2nd edn). Boston: Allyn & Bacon.

Matson JL, Mayville EA (2001) The relationship of functional variables and psychopathology to aggressive behavior in persons with severe and profound mental retardation. Journal of Psychopathology & Behavioral Assessment 23: 3–9.

Matson JL, Mulick JA (1991) Handbook of Mental Retardation (2nd edn). New York: Pergamon Press.

Matson JL, Anderson SJ, Bamburg JW (2000) The relationship of social skills to psychopathology for individuals with mild and moderate mental retardation. British Journal of Developmental Disabilities 46: 15–22.

Matson JL, Smiroldo BB, Bamburg JW (1998) The relationship of social skills to psychopathology for individuals with severe or profound mental retardation. Journal of Intellectual and Developmental Disability 23: 137–45.

Matson JL, Bamburg JW, Mayville EA, Khan I (1999) Seizure disorders in people with intellectual disability: an analysis of differences in social functioning, adaptive functioning and maladaptive behaviours. Journal of Intellectual Disability Research 43: 531–9.

Meadow KP, Schlesinger HS (1971) The prevalence of behavioral problems in a population of deaf school children. American Annals of the Deaf 116: 346–8.

Mental Health Aspects of Developmental Disabilities (1998–present) Bear Creek, NC: Psych-Media, Inc.

Mirenda P (1997) Supporting individuals with challenging behavior through functional communication training and AAC: research review. Augmentative and Alternative Communication 13: 207–25.

Mitchell TV, Quittner AL (1996) Multimethod study of attention and behavior problems in hearing-impaired children. Journal of Clinical Child Psychology 25: 83–96.

Mudford OC (1995) Review of the gentle teaching data. American Journal on Mental Retardation 99: 345–55.

Murphy G, Hall S, Oliver C, Kissi-Debra R (1999) Identification of early self-injurious behaviour in young children with intellectual disability. Journal of Intellectual Disability Research 43: 149–63.

Murphy G, MacDonald S, Hall S, Oliver C (2000) Aggression and the termination of "rituals": a new variant of the escape function for challenging behavior. Research in Developmental Disabilities 21: 43–59.

Murphy G, Oliver C, Corbett J et al. (1993) Epidemiology of self-injury, characteristics of people with severe self-injury and initial treatment outcome. In C Kiernan (ed.), Research to Practice? Implications of Research on Challenging Behaviour of People with Learning Disability (pp. 1–35). Avon: British Institute of Learning Disabilities.

Oliver C, Murphy GH, Corbett JA (1987) Self-injurious behaviour in people with mental handicap: a total population study. Journal of Mental Deficiency Research 31: 147–62.

Olson B, Rett A (1985) Behavioral observations concerning differential diagnosis between Rett Syndrome and autism. Brain and Development 6: 281–9.

O'Reilly MF (1995) Functional analysis and treatment of escape-maintained aggression correlated with sleep deprivation. Journal of Applied Behavior Analysis 28: 225–6.

O'Reilly MF (1997) Functional analysis of episodic self-injury correlated with recurrent otitis media. Journal of Applied Behavior Analysis 30: 165–7.

O'Reilly MF (1999) Effects of pre-session attention on the frequency of attention-maintained behavior. Journal of Applied Behavior Analysis 32: 371–4.

O'Reilly MF, Lancioni GE (2000) Response covariation of escape-maintained aberrant behavior correlated with sleep deprivation. Research in Developmental Disabilities 21:125–6.

O'Reilly MF, Lacey C, Lancioni G (2000) Assessment of the influence of background noise on escape-maintained problem behavior and pain behavior in a child with Williams Syndrome. Journal of Applied Behavior Analysis 33: 511–14.

Orelove FP, Sobsey D (eds) (1996) Educating Children with Multiple Disabilities: A Transdisciplinary Approach (2nd edn). Baltimore: Paul H. Brookes Publishing Co.

Paclawskyj TR, Matson JL, Rush KS et al. (2000) Questions About Behavioral Function (QABF): a behavioral checklist for functional assessment of aberrant behavior. Research in Developmental Disabilities 21: 223–9.

Parmenter TR (1994) Quality of life as a concept and measurable entity. Social Indicators Research 33: 9–46.

Parmenter TR, Einfeld S, Tonge B, Dempster JA (1998) Behavioural and emotional problems in the classroom of children and adolescents with intellectual disability. Journal of Intellectual and Developmental Disability 23: 71–7.

Pearpoint J, Forest M, O'Brien J (1996) MAPs, Circles of Friends, and PATH: powerful tools to help build caring communities. In S Stainback, W Stainback (eds), Inclusion: A Guide for Educators (pp. 67–86). Baltimore: Paul H. Brookes Publishing Co.

Positive Behavioral Interventions and Supports (PBIS), http://pbis.org/ accessed 22 November 2002.

Pyles D, Bailey J (1992) Behavioral diagnostic interventions. In JK Luiselli, JL Matson, N Singh (eds), Self-injurious Behavior: Analysis, Assessment, and Treatment (pp. 155–80). Berlin: Springer-Verlag.

Qureshi H (1994) The size of the problem. In E Emerson, P McGill, J Mansell (eds), Severe Learning Disabilities and Challenging Behaviours (pp. 17–36). London: Chapman & Hall.

Qureshi H, Alborz A (1992) Epidemiology of challenging behaviour. Mental Handicap Research 5: 130–45.

Ranzon B (2001) The impact of anxiety on challenging behavior. Developmental Disabilities Bulletin 29: 97–112.

Reber M, Borcherding BG (1997) Dual diagnosis: mental retardation and psychiatric disorders. In ML Batshaw (ed.), Children with Disabilities (4th edn) (pp. 405–24). Baltimore: Paul H. Brookes Publishing Co.

Reese MR (1997) Biobehavior analysis of self-injurious behavior in a person with profound handicaps. Focus on Autism and Other Developmental Disabilities 12: 87–94.

Reid R, Maag JW (1998) Functional assessment: a method for developing classroom-based accommodations and interventions for children with ADHD. Reading and Writing Quarterly 14: 9–42.

Reiss S (1993) Assessment of psychopathology in persons with mental retardation. In JL Matson, RB Barrett (eds), Psychopathology in the Mentally Retarded (2nd edn) (pp. 17–40). Boston: Allyn & Bacon.

Remington B (1996) Assessing the occurrence of learning in children with profound intellectual disability: a conditioning approach. International Journal of Disability, Development & Education 43: 101–18

Risley T (1996) Get a life!: positive behavioral intervention for challenging behavior through life arrangement and life coaching. In LK Koegel, RL Koegel, G Dunlap (eds), Positive Behavioural Support: Including People with Difficult Behavior in the Community (pp. 425–37). Baltimore: Paul H. Brookes Publishing Co.

Robbins FR, Dunlap G (1992) Effects of task difficulty on parent teaching skills and behavior problems of young children with autism. American Journal on Mental Retardation 96: 631–43.

Russell O, Harris P (1993) Assessing the prevalence of aggressive behaviour and the effectiveness of interventions. In C Kiernan (ed.), Research to Practice? Implications of Research on Challenging Behaviour of People with Learning Disability (pp. 37–52). Avon: British Institute of Learning Disabilities.

Rutter M (1989) Isle of Wight revisited: twenty-five years of child psychiatric epidemiology. Journal of the American Academy of Child and Adolescent Psychiatry 28: 633–53.

Schalock RL (2000) Three decades of quality of life. Focus on Autism and Other Developmental Disabilities 15(2): 116–27.

Schnittjer CJ, Hirshoren A (1981) The prevalence of behavior problems in deaf children. Psychology in the Schools 18: 67–72.

Schroeder SR, Schroeder CS, Smith B, Dalldorf J (1978) Prevalence of self-injurious behaviors in a large state facility for the retarded: a three-year follow-up study. Journal of Autism and Childhood Schizophrenia 8: 261–9.

Schroeder SR, Tessel RE, Loupe PS, Stodgell CJ (1997) Severe behavior problems among people with developmental disabilities. In WE MacLean Jr (ed.), Ellis' Handbook of Mental Deficiency, Psychological Theory and Research (3rd edn) (pp. 439–64). Mahwah, NJ: Lawrence Erlbaum.

Scott TM, Nelson CM (1999) Functional behavioral assessment: implications for training and staff development. Behavioral Disorders 24: 249–52.

Scott TM, DeSimone C, Fowler W, Webb E (2000) Using functional assessment to develop interventions for challenging behaviors in the classroom: three case studies. Preventing School Failure 44: 51–8.

Sharma S, Sigafoos J, Carroll A (2002) Challenging behaviour among Indian children with visual impairment. British Journal of Visual Impairment 20: 4–6.

Siegel-Causey E, Bashinski SM (1997) Enhancing initial communication and responsiveness of learners with multiple disabilities: a tri-focus framework for partners. Focus on Autism and Other Developmental Disabilities 12: 105–20.

Sigafoos J (1997) A review of communication intervention programs for people with developmental disabilities. Behaviour Change 14: 125–38.

Sigafoos J (2000) Communication development and aberrant behavior in children with developmental disabilities. Education and Training in Mental Retardation and Developmental Disabilities 35: 168–76.

Sigafoos J, Pennell D (1995) Parent and teacher assessment of receptive and expressive language in preschool children with developmental disabilities. Education and Training in Mental Retardation and Developmental Disabilities 30: 329–35.

Sigafoos J, Einfeld S, Parmenter TR (2001) An introduction to challenging behaviour in children with intellectual disabilities. Special Education Perspectives 10(2): 37–46.

Sigafoos J, Pennell D, Versluis J (1996) Naturalistic assessment leading to effective treatment of self-injury in a young boy with multiple disabilities. Education and Treatment of Children 19: 101–23.

Sigafoos J, Elkins J, Kerr M, Attwood T (1994) A survey of aggressive behaviour among a population of persons with intellectual disability in Queensland. Journal of Intellectual Disability Research 38: 369–81.

Sigafoos J, Tucker M, Bushell H, Webber Y (1997) A practical strategy to increase participation and reduce challenging behavior during leisure skills programming. Mental Retardation 35: 198–208.

Singer GHS, Gert B, Koegel RL (1999) A moral framework for analysing the controversy over aversive behavioral interventions for people with severe mental retardation. Journal of Positive Behavior Interventions 1: 88–100.

Skinner BF (1945) The operational analysis of psychological terms. Psychological Review 52: 270–7.

Skinner BF (1953) Science and Human Behavior. New York: Macmillan.

Skinner BF (1968) The Technology of Teaching. New York: Appleton-Century-Crofts.

Smith T, Groen AD, Wynn JW (2000) Randomized trial of intensive early intervention for children with pervasive developmental disorder. American Journal on Mental Retardation 105: 269–85.

Sobsey D (1994) Violence and Abuse in the Lives of People with Disabilities: The End of Silent Acceptance? Baltimore: Paul H. Brookes Publishing Co.

Sobsey D, Thuppal M (1996) Children with special health care needs. In FP Orelove, D Sobsey (eds), Educating Children with Multiple Disabilities: A Transdisciplinary Approach (2nd edn) (pp. 161–216). Baltimore: Paul H. Brookes Publishing Co.

Stephenson JR, Dowrick M (2000) Parent priorities in communication intervention for young students with severe disabilities. Education and Training in Mental Retardation and Developmental Disabilities 35: 25–35.

Strain PS (2001) Empirically based social skill intervention: a case for quality-of-life improvement. Behavioral Disorders 27: 30–6.

Strain PS, Kohler FW (1998) Peer-mediated social intervention for young children with autism. Seminars in Speech and Language 19: 391–405.

Strain PS, McGee G, Kohler FW (2000) Inclusion of children with autism in early intervention: an examination of rationale, myths, and procedures. In MJ Guralnick (ed.), Early Childhood Inclusion: Focus on Change (pp. 308–36). Baltimore: Paul H. Brookes Publishing Co.

Sturmey P, Vernon J (2001) Administrative prevalence of autism in the Texas school system. Journal of the American Academy of Child & Adolescent Psychiatry 40: 621.

Sugai G, Horner RH, Sprague JR (1999) Functional-assessment-based behavior support planning: research to practice to research. Behavioral Disorders 24: 253–7.

Symons FJ, Butler MG, Sanders MD et al. (1999) Self-injurious behavior and Prader-Willi Syndrome: behavioral forms and body locations. American Journal on Mental Retardation 104: 260–9.

Thompson T (1977) Behavior Modification of the Mentally Retarded (2nd edn). New York: Oxford University Press.

Thompson T, Axtell S, Schaal D (1993) Self-injurious behavior: mechanisms and intervention. In JL Matson, RB Barrett (eds), Psychopathology in the Mentally Retarded (2nd edn) (pp. 179–211). Boston: Allyn & Bacon.

Tohill C (1997) A study into the possible link between antiepileptic drugs and the risk of fractures in Muckamore Abbey Hospital. Journal of Intellectual & Developmental Disability 22: 281–92.

Tohill C, Laverty A (2001) Sunshine, diet and mobility for healthy bones – an intervention study designed to implement these standards into the daily routine in an at risk population of adults with intellectual disability. Journal of Intellectual & Developmental Disability 26: 217–31.

Tonge BJ, Einfeld SL (1991) Intellectual disability and psychopathology in Australian children. Australia and New Zealand Journal of Developmental Disabilities 17: 155–67.

Touchette P, McDonald R, Langer S (1985) A scatterplot for identifying stimulus control of problem behavior. Journal of Applied Behavior Analysis 18: 343–51.

Tucker M, Sigafoos J, Bushell H (1998) Use of noncontingent reinforcement in the treatment of challenging behavior: a review and clinical guide. Behavior Modification 22: 529–47.

Turnbull A, Edmonson H, Griggs P et al. (2002) A blueprint for schoolwide positive behavior support: implementation of three components. Exceptional Children 68: 377–402.

Turnbull HR, Wilcox BL, Stowe M et al. (2000) Public policy foundations for positive behavioral interventions, strategies, and supports. Journal of Positive Behavior Interventions 2: 218–30.

van Eldik T (1994) Behavior problems with deaf Dutch boys. American Annals of the Deaf 139: 394–9.

van Eldik T, Veerman JW, Treffers FD, Verhulst FC (2000) Problem behaviour and the family environment of deaf children [Dutch]. Kind en Adolescent 21: 232–51.

Van Hasselt VB, Kazdin AE, Hersen M (1986) Assessment of problem behaviors in visually handicapped adolescents. Journal of Clinical Child Psychology 15: 134–41.

Van Houten R, Axelrod S, Bailey JS et al. (1988) The right to effective behavioral treatment. The Behavior Analyst 11: 381–4.

Vandercook T, York J, Forest M (1989) The McGill action planning system (MAPS): a strategy for building the vision. Journal of the Association for Persons with Severe Handicaps 14: 79–87.

Vittemberga GL, Scotti JR, Weigle KL (1999) Standards of practice and critical elements in an educative approach to behavioral intervention. In JR Scotti, LH Meyer (eds), Behavioral Intervention: Principles, Models, and Practices (pp. 47–69). Baltimore: Paul H. Brookes Publishing Co.

Vostanis P, Hayes M, Du Feu M, Warren J (1997) Detection of behavioural and emotional problems in deaf children and adolescents: comparison of two rating scales. Child Care, Health & Development 23: 233–46.

Wacker DP, Peck S, Derby KM et al. (1996) Developing long-term reciprocal interactions between parents and their young children with problematic behavior. In LK Koegel, RL Koegel, G Dunlap (eds), Positive Behavioral Support: Including People with Difficult Behavior in the Community (pp. 51–80). Baltimore: Paul H. Brookes.

Walker HM, Colvin G, Ramsey E (1995) Antisocial Behavior in School: Strategies and Best Practices. Pacific Grove, CA: Brooks/Cole.

Wehmeyer ML (1999) A functional model of self-determination: describing development and implementing instruction. Focus on Autism and Other Developmental Disabilities 14: 53–61.

Wehmeyer M, Bersani H, Gagne R (2000) Riding the third wave: self-determination and self-advocacy in the 21st century. Focus on Autism and Other Developmental Disabilities 15: 106–15.

Weiss N (2002) Stop! There's a baby in that bath water: embracing the critical value of communication and facilitated communication. TASH Connections 28(5): 3–4.

Westling DL, Fox L (2000) Teaching Students with Severe Disabilities (2nd edn). Columbus, OH: Merrill.

Winchel RM, Stanley M (1991) Self-injurious behavior: a review of the behavior and biology of self-mutilation. American Journal of Psychiatry 148: 306–17.

Wing L, Attwood A (1987) Syndromes of autism and atypical development. In DJ Cohen, A Donnellan, R Paul (eds), Handbook of Autism and Pervasive Developmental Disorders (pp. 3–19). Silver Springs, MD: Winston.

Woermann FG, van Elst LT, Koepp MJ et al. (2000) Reduction of frontal neocortical grey matter associated with affective aggression in patients with temporal lobe epilepsy: an objective voxel by voxel analysis of automatically segmented MRI. Journal of Neurology, Neurosurgery, and Psychiatry 68: 162–9.

Young AT, Hawkins J (2002) Psychotropic medication prescriptions: an analysis of the reasons people with mental retardation are prescribed psychotropic medication. Journal of Developmental and Physical Disabilities 14: 129–42.

Young L, Ashman A, Sigafoos J, Grevell P (2001) Closure of the Challinor Centre II: an extended report on 95 individuals after 12 months of community living. Journal of Intellectual and Developmental Disability 26: 51–66.

Young L, Sigafoos J, Suttie J et al. (1998) Deinstitutionalisation of persons with intellectual disability: a review of Australian studies. Journal of Intellectual and Developmental Disability 23: 155–70.

Index